The Boniface Option

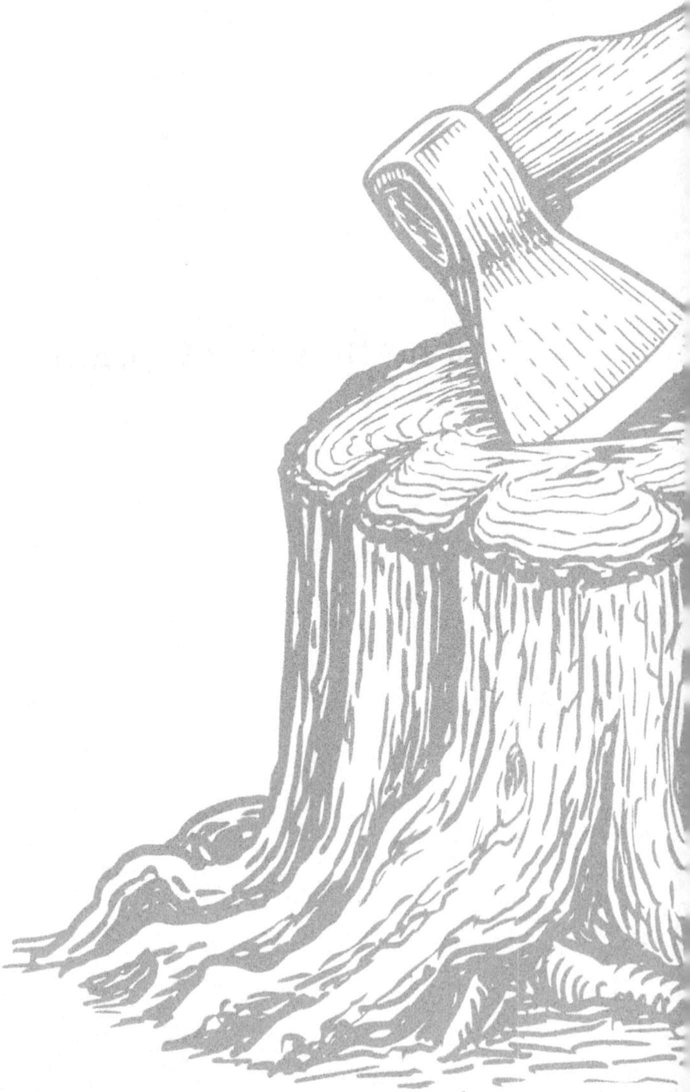

The
BONIFACE
OPTION

A Strategy for Christian Counteroffensive in a Post-Christian Nation

ANDREW ISKER

gab

CLARKS SUMMIT
PENNSYLVANIA

Published by Gab AI Inc
Clarks Summit, Pennsylvania
www.gab.com

Andrew Isker, *The Boniface Option: A Strategy for Christian Counteroffensive in a Post-Christian Nation*
Copyright © 2023 by Andrew Isker.

Cover design and illustration by Emerson.
Interior layout and ebook conversion by Valerie Anne Bost.

Unless otherwise noted, all Scripture quotations are from the New King James Version®. Copyright © 1982 by Thomas Nelson. Used by permission. All rights reserved. Quotations marked KJV are from the King James Version, public domain.

All rights reserved. No part of this publication may be reproduced, stored in a retrieval system, or transmitted in any form by any means, electronic, mechanical, photocopy, recording, or otherwise, without prior permission of the author, except as provided by USA copyright law.

23 24 25 26 27 28 29 30 31 32   10 9 8 7 6 5 4 3 2 1

For Kara,
my beloved wife
and the mother of my many future Bonifaces.

Contents

Preface ix

Introduction 1

Part One: Chopping Down the Idols of Trashworld

1   Disenchantment with the Modern World 11

2   Economic Emasculation 21

3   Atomized Man 33

4   Biological Castration 47

5   Jezebel 57

6   Bugmen in the Cocoon 69

Part Two: Transforming the Felled Trees of Trashworld into a New Christendom

7	The Bedrock for a New Christendom	79
8	Masculine Economics	91
9	Brotherhood	107
10	Made for War	117
11	A New Eve	127
12	The Paideia of Christendom	137

Conclusion. 145
Acknowledgments. 163

Preface

Trashworld

You live in a dystopia.

Every part of historical human existence in our world has been turned on its head. The world we live in is an inversion of what God created you to live in. All that is good is treated as though it were repugnant. All that is beautiful is treated as though it were repulsive. And the truth is forbidden while the most outrageous lies are exalted. This world did not become like this by accident or by inexorable forces of history. This world was engineered to be this way. It was designed to take the life your ancestors had and tear it apart to prevent you from attaining a normal, human way of life.

After the events of 2020, the lockdowns, the Regime-sponsored riots, and the dubious election, many people became aware of the fact that we have elites who rule over us who might not have our best interests in mind. For at least a segment of the population, the World Economic Forum, Klaus Schwab, George Soros, and the late Jeffrey Epstein became household names. Many people have rightly begun to fear the designs such people have for our world. "I will not eat the bugs; I will not live in the pod" became a popular internet meme. Millions of people are now terrified of what apocalyptic hellscape these people will create.

But they are not asking the right questions.

The question is not "what are they planning to do to us?" What you should be asking is "what have they already done? And what can people do about it?"

The insane, dystopian and totalitarian world we fear the elites might create is one we *already live* in.

If you were to describe life today to men of a century ago, they would think you must be insane. "People have their genitals removed and live as the opposite sex?" "They also do this to children?" "Homosexuality is treated as totally normal and is even celebrated?" "No one is able to recognize the differences between men and women?" "The same President Taft who got stuck in his bathtub would look skinny compared to the average person in your day?" "No one has any real friendships, and they are isolated and separated from their extended families and places of their birth?" "You can be made permanently unemployable if you oppose any of this publicly?"

Our ancestors would instantly recognize that you shouldn't fear the world the elites *might* one day bring about; you should be alarmed at the one they already *did* bring about.

This isn't to say that they cannot make things much worse. The tens of millions imprisoned, tortured, and starved to death by the totalitarianism of the Soviet Union and Mao's China are an example of what could certainly happen. We should be wary of what they could do. But far too often what *could* happen masks what has *already* occurred.

We are already in the midst of decades of social engineering. The society we have is already an anti-human one. It is already one designed to remove from you all that made life meaningful and fulfilling. It has torn you from people and place. It is designed to make you isolated, lonely, and, above all else, totally docile.

Throughout the pages of this book, I use the term *Trashworld* to describe this dystopian society.

And the point of *The Boniface Option* is to make you see it for what it is and to begin the hard work of escaping and overcoming it.

Fake and Gay

Another phrase you will find in the pages of this book is *fake and gay*. What may seem like a transgressive, sophomoric internet pejorative has far more meaning than you may think. Trashworld is inherently not real. It is a massive, revolutionary superstructure made possible by the technological progress and the material abundance of industrial society which allows a society to continue to function despite running 180 degrees from the created order. The reason something like Trashworld never came into being in the pre-modern world is that without the unprecedented wealth created by industrialism, such a civilization would immediately collapse. The fakeness of Trashworld can therefore seem to keep going indefinitely because the social fabric required to keep a premodern civilization functioning economically has been at least temporarily bypassed by unparalleled industrial production. To those who rule over us, human-scaled life is no longer necessary. If anything, to them, it is an obstacle.

The gayness of "fake and gay" is not merely some schoolyard slur. There is deep meaning to this, too. The homosexual is not just a sexual deviant. His very nature and the very center of his identity is a man whose urges take precedence over all else. In the 1980s, as the AIDS epidemic was at its height, the leftist French philosopher Michel Foucault nevertheless continued to regularly attend bathhouse orgies and homosexual sado-masochistic clubs. He famously wrote, "Sex is worth dying for." He meant what he said. He died of AIDS in 1984.

For the homosexual, insatiable desires must be pursued even knowing it will cost him his life. In economic terms, he is the ultimate high-time-preference man. He only lives in the present. There is no thought for the future. He is quite obviously incapable of pursuing offspring. He is willing to cut off any and all social relations that prevent him from pursuing his predilections. In short, the homosexual is both the apex consumer and the easiest personality to manipulate and lord over.

Therefore the gayness of Trashworld is our rulers' social engineering of the population to create the exact same ethos of the homosexual in everyone, regardless of their sexual tastes. They want you to be *spiritually* homosexual whether or not they can make you *actually* homosexual. They want everyone uprooted and alone. They want you to be only concerned with satisfying your immediate desires. They do not want you to care about the future. They do not want you to have children. They want your entire purpose in life to be "Consume today, for tomorrow we die."

In escaping and resisting Trashworld, you must first see all the ways in which the "fake and gay" pervades all of life. There is nowhere you can run to and hide from it. You can only confront and overcome it. That willingness to confront it in yourself and in the world around you is the spirit of *The Boniface Option*.

Introduction

The Story of Saint Boniface

At the height of Rome's imperial glory she attempted, for centuries, to subdue the peoples beyond the Rhine. No matter how many legions they devoted to the task, the fierceness of these warrior people was too much to overcome. Rome had destroyed the powerful empire of Carthage, she had subdued all of Gaul, she had taken Greece and nearly all the lands of Alexander's domain. She had turned the Mediterranean Sea into a Roman lake. But she could not subdue Germania.

Rome had made many incursions across the Rhine. There had been brief periods where German chieftains had been made vassals, their sons given to be hostages and Romanized. One such was named Arminius, who led a revolt against Rome about the same year the boy Jesus was teaching in the Temple in Luke 2. Arminius betrayed his Roman benefactors and united the tribes to reject their Roman yoke. When the tribute stopped coming, the legions under Quintilius Varus were dispatched. Arminius, educated in all the ways of Rome, particularly her military tactics, led three Roman legions into a trap in the Teutoburg Forest. Of the 20,000 Roman troops, not a single one escaped with his life. Suetonius reports that when Augustus learned of the disaster, he repeatedly cried out "Varus, give me back my legions."

Germania had ended Roman imperial expansion, and centuries later other Germanics, the Goths, would snuff out Roman imperial glory for good. To say these were a fierce people would be an understatement.

And it was to these unconquerable people, an ambitious Saxon monk from the Order of St. Benedict, Winfred, was called to preach the victory of Jesus Christ in 716. When Winfrid's abbot died that year, rather than succeed him and enjoy the secure and relatively comfortable life leading the monastery, he left the safety of that monastery to preach to ferocious Germanic pagans in Frisia.

After a pilgrimage to Rome in 718, Winfrid was renamed "Boniface" by Pope Gregory II and commissioned to convert Germania to the Christian religion. Despite the expansion of the Frankish kingdom's domain across the Rhine, Germania remained thoroughly pagan, even if Christianity had begun to gain tacit acceptance.

If there was any acceptance of Christ among the Germanics, He was merely added to the pantheon of Norse gods rather than replacing them. The Germanics continued to offer sacrifices to Odin and Thor, examine the entrails of sacrificial victims, cast runes and other divination, practice sorcery and dark incantations. In short, Germania was still ruled by demons. Into this world, stepped Boniface.

After preaching the gospel and slowly gaining converts among the Germanics, Boniface traveled to the great pagan shrine in Geismar in Hesse. There at Donar's Oak, the pagan priests offered sacrifices to their demon-god, Donar, better known to us as Thor, the same ancient storm demon named Jupiter among the Romans, Zeus among the Greeks, and Baal among the Canaanites.

It was believed that if anyone profaned Thor's oak by touching it, the demon would strike that man down with a bolt of lightning from his hammer. When Boniface arrived at the tree, he told the pagan priests that he would return at the same time tomorrow, and not only would he touch this tree, he would cut it down.

Word traveled quickly throughout the neighboring villages and towns. A great multitude arrived the next day, brimming with excitement to see their god fry this foolish and blasphemous Christian. Boniface reared back with his ax and took one, single swing, barely bruising the bark of the mighty tree, when a powerful wind came out of the heavens and blew the tree over. Astonished to see the impotence of their demon-god, everyone present forsook their paganism and was baptized into Jesus Christ.

From here, the Word began to flourish in Germania. Boniface faithfully preached the gospel and taught the ways of Christ to the Germanics, but his greatest feat was organizing the newly forming Germanic church. Converts continued to flow in and pagan shrines all over Germania were sacked and replaced with churches, the greatest need was building a network of churches that could minister to these new Christians and disciple them. This may seem mundane compared to the mighty deed in the felling of Donar's Oak, but anyone who has ever been involved in the administrative tasks of the church can tell you, successfully setting up a massive bishopric that functions well is a feat worthy of mention—all without email.

Boniface dedicated his life to the evangelization and discipleship of Germany and after seeing thousands of pagans turn to Christ, he now desired to continue the evangelization of the Frisians in the north, where his ministry had started forty years earlier. Nearly eighty years old, Boniface knew the journey would likely claim his life, and so, among his books and other few important possessions, he packed his linen burial shroud.

He made it to Frisia with a large retinue, and preached the gospel with some success. But his time there was cut short. For he and his entourage were attacked by bandits. These robbers hoped to find gold in the chests and luggage of Boniface but instead found something worthless to them: several large codexes. It was here, holding up one of these books containing God's very words, that Boniface received the martyr's crown of glory.

Overcoming the Post-Christian Dark Age

I'm writing this book in *Anno Domini* 2023 and I can confidently say that we live in a new dark age. An age similar in many ways to the world of St. Boniface. You may not have noticed, but the great empire that rules the world is in a state of collapse. And not just starting in 2020, this collapse has been ongoing for the better part of a century and could continue on for just as long. This collapse, like the collapse of most empires, takes place over several generations before anyone even realizes what has happened. It is like Hemingway's famous saying about how he went bankrupt "first gradually, then suddenly." Decline is usually imperceptible, like the minute hand on a clock. Unless you are looking very closely, you don't notice it moving, but then all of a sudden you look up and an hour has slipped away. Our society recently experienced a look up at the clock, a Hemingway's "suddenly," in 2020. Whatever else we may say about it, and there is a great deal to say about it, the COVID-19 Pandemic was a revelatory experience. It didn't produce all that much that was new, but it *did* pull back the curtain revealing everything that was already there.

Anyone with eyes to see, saw firsthand that all the gods of the modern world are as impotent as Thor before the ax of Boniface. The medical-pharmaceutical-bureaucratic complex was powerless to stop a weaponized cold, or (more likely) far too corrupt and inept to identify a coherent strategy to mitigate it. The state, which fancies itself omnipotent, wielded tyrannical power in a vain utopian quest to stop a virus by halting all of society, locking them in their homes, and then, when this failed, forcing humiliation garments on every human face. None of the utopian fantasies of the modern liberal state were able to do anything but increase human misery. And lastly, it was revealed just how many churches will give into hysteria, forsake worshiping for months or even years, all to receive the approval of a society that increasingly hates them.

Ours is a society that went from a space-faring people two generations ago to one that cannot even keep aircraft carriers from destroying themselves while at port.[1] We have gone from one where a married mom and dad could own a home and enjoy a decent middle class life for their children to one where few are married, fewer still can afford a home, and we have to go out of our way to pass laws to keep teachers from grooming our children into having their genitalia removed.

It has become obvious that we are in a period of steep decline—politically, economically, culturally, and above all else, spiritually. In 2017, in the wake of the *Obergefell*

---

1. In July 2020, the Wasp-class amphibious assault ship *USS Bonhomme Richard* caught fire while docked in San Diego and was so badly damaged she had to be scuttled.

decision codifying sodomites as a protected class in the United States, Rod Dreher published *The Benedict Option*. This book, comparing the current situation in the West to Europe at the start of the Dark Age was a massive hit. Most of the Christian world had not yet reconciled that the culture war had been lost; Christian civilization had finally been repudiated in the public square, a secular, liberal, democratic morality had emerged triumphant, and Dreher was among the first with a large audience to declare what we should do next. His book plotted a course for what had been done previously, when Rome had fallen, the remnants of civilization were held together by intentional Christian communities dedicated to preserving Christian civilization, a movement begun by St. Benedict in the sixth century. It was a helpful analogy, tactical withdrawal to refuges of strength to rebuild Christian civilization.

The problem with Dreher's thesis is the analogy isn't adequate. The West is indeed in a state of collapse as noted above, but rather than being sacked by Goths, we have been consumed internally by an insane and suicidal death cult. Instead of Alaric at the head of the Gothic army, it is Vladimir Lenin in high heels. As the West very slowly descends into the maelstrom, the power of the ruling regime has not lessened at all, and worse, their willingness to wield this power against their enemies has increased. Withdrawal to rebuild in places of strength works in a post-Roman, medieval Mad Max scenario, but it does not work when the dying empire is still intact and ruled by the kind of people who make Nero seem responsible and judicious.

In a world such as this, a world which is a blend of America, Ancient Rome, the Soviet Union, and the worst parts of the *Blade Runner* dystopia, we will not be allowed to withdraw to the monasteries. We instead must actively and boldly oppose the apostasy of the West. Nothing short of courageous opposition to the Trashworld of the apostate West will do. The Benedict Option is not available to us; it is either the Boniface Option or destruction. You cannot run and hide from Trashworld. Our only option is to despise it and to fight back.

PART ONE
Chopping Down the Idols of Trashworld

CHAPTER 1

Disenchantment with the Modern World

A time to love,
And a time to hate;
A time of war,
And a time of peace.

ECCLESIASTES 3:8

You must learn what to hate. If you are an evangelical Christian, like me, you have been trained your entire life to recoil at such a thing. God is love, after all. It is not Christlike to hate, you have been told. But this is simply not true. To love a thing is to hate its opposite. I love the innocence and purity of children; therefore I utterly hate pedophilia. I love my wife; therefore I hate to see her mistreated. For far too long, the evangelical Christian has been told he may not hate anything. He may only love. The schoolmarm is always over his shoulder telling him, "If you have nothing nice to say, don't say anything at all." We are trained to not love as we ought because we are trained to never hate. "That's very hateful" is the bane of the neutered evangelical. It is the very worst thing you can say to him. He will instantly shrink and begin apologizing. But to love a thing is inherently to hate its opposite. *Indifference* is the absence of love, not hatred. Where love is present you will axiomatically have hatred of the object of that love's opposite. If the Christian has a passionate love for the truth of God's Word, the goodness of God's justice, and the beauty of holiness, he will necessarily have an intense hatred of the lies, injustice, and sin.

When one of the multitude of goblins from the occupational regime on the Potomac speaks about spreading "our values" to the nations of the former Soviet Bloc, such as Ukraine, what do they mean by that? Naturally, language such as this is meaningless boilerplate to them. These are throwaway lines recited by brainless automatons. But they speak them because they know they mean something to us or at least they used to. What are "our values"? You would probably say something like "freedom and democracy." And that is, more or less, what they are trying to evoke. But there again, what do they mean by those words? What Kamala Harris or Anthony Blinken says freedom and democracy are is not the same as what a 58-year-old farmer in Keota, Iowa, might think they are.

For normal American people, this is their heritage. This is what their fathers and grandfathers and great-grandfathers shed their blood to defend. The freedom to speak your mind, the freedom to elect your rulers, the freedom to worship your God, the freedom to defend your family. And *democracy* means the people of a nation get a say in their own governance. If you go to a GOP caucus in a rural county, you will hear the words *freedom* and *democracy* thrown around a lot. But the meaning those words hold for the average conservative American is far different than apparatchiks on the Potomac.

But the regime also knows this as well and has hollowed them out and wears them as a skin suit. When Joe Biden or Hillary Clinton goes on TV to talk about defending "our values" from Vladimir Putin, they want electricians in Bismarck, North Dakota, or plumbers in Leesburg, Florida, with "Let's Go Brandon" stickers on their F–150s to think, "Yes, we must make sure those poor Ukrainians get to enjoy freedom of religion and freedom of speech and are able to live under leaders of their choosing." But that is not at all what "our values" actually are.

What they mean by "our values" is a world where human beings are divorced as much as they possibly can be from God's creation and created order so that they can be fit subjects for modern liberal consumerist society. They want to take relatively impoverished traditional societies, many of which have already suffered greatly under Bolshevism and Stalinism, and strip away their heritage, their rootedness to their homes and villages and families, and whatever traditional morality and Christian religion survived Communist rule so as to assimilate them into the Borg Collective, where they will be trained to wait alone in their pods, consuming terabytes of porn while they wait for the next Marvel movie to come out. *That* is the "freedom and democracy" our regime seeks to spread. *That* is the "freedom and democracy" they believe Americans cherish. *That* is "our values."

The Small-Souled Bugman

That soulless dystopia is the society that our rulers have engineered. They want children stripped away from loyalty to their parents as much as possible, which they accomplish through public education. Loyalty to parents is severed, and loyalty to (usually) popular culture is mediated through peers or, in the worst cases, the ideology of the regime mediated through teachers is established. From there, most go to college to be physically separated from their parents totally, in addition to being spiritually and emotionally severed. There they are presented with a Pleasure Island where hedonism and sexual exploration are the carrot to the stick of ideological cajoling by leftist, anti-Christian faculty. The individual, who was once part of an organic whole, part of a family, a people, and a place, is now separated and stripped bare of all other loyalties and loves and made a *tabula rasa*, a willing vessel for the religion and culture of the globohomo world order.

From here, he is released into the wild. He takes a job filling a space in a cubicle, filling a spreadsheet and sending emails until he drives home, in a sea of cars full of lonely people just like him on the freeway, until he gets to his home, fills his belly with industrial slop delivered by Door Dash, watches porn, browses social media (especially Reddit), plays Xbox, or binges a show until he goes to sleep to repeat the process all over again.

This man has been reduced to a bug in a hive. He is something less than a human being. He is a drone, waiting in his pod until it is time to fulfill his duties as a member of the hive. The things that give his life meaning are all products for him to consume, products that give him a temporary dopamine rush, that sustains the meaninglessness of what his life has become. He is divorced from all other meaning, he is isolated from meaningful human relationships, and his moral formation has been shaped by pop culture. Such a person can be easily manipulated, reduced to his baser appetites. Whatever he must do or believe to preserve his comforts he will do.

It therefore should come as no surprise that the Wuhan flu lockdowns were so readily embraced by these types. If you are already conditioned to enjoy life inside a twelve-by-twelve cell so long as you have enough anesthetizing, consumerist products, you will submit to any slavery that provides this to you. Even more so when indulging your pathetic appetites can be celebrated as a virtue! He is dehumanized, reduced to an animal in a cage.

The moral formation of these people is shaped almost entirely by the entertainment industry from infancy. What a person believes is true, good, and beautiful is not shaped by what their church teaches, or their parents and grandparents hand down to them, or even what their nation holds in common; the heart of the modern denizen of the post-war, liberal consumerist order is shaped by film and recording studios. From before he could speak until he became an adult, he has watched tens of thousands of sermons shaping and forming his heart to love Trashworld. We don't recognize them as sermons because we think they are religiously neutral TV shows and movies, but they are fundamentally not mere entertainment, but religious training. Here you are trained to believe that all of those that came before you were stupid, close-minded, bigoted, barbaric, and superstitious. All of Chesterton's fences are torn down; every tradition that formed you both as an individual and member of a people or nation is either removed or looked upon with deep suspicion. You are trained to believe you are a total blank slate. All your beliefs, everything your heart holds to be true, good, and beautiful, you believe you have formed as a totally independent, free-thinker (when, in reality, they have been carefully crafted by insidious social engineers to make you the apex consumer). If you reverse-engineer the beliefs of the average modern man you would have to conclude that someone intentional designed him to be that way, a man who lives by the rule, "Don't ask questions, just consume product and then get excited for next products." It cannot be overstated how much this must be at the center of the church's apologetics. The modern man will say he wants rational proof or evidence that the Bible is true, but the reality is that he does not. He may even think he is sincere when he demands such things from the Christian, but the fact of the matter is apologetic arguments in the post-war, liberal, consumerist West are not about whether or not you can make a strong rational argument for the existence of God or provide enough evidence to the unbeliever that the Bible is true and trustworthy. While obviously useful, arguments do not matter in this culture clash. If someone's moral formation is designed to make them impervious to the truths of Scripture, no amount of even the most brilliant apologetic argument will persuade them to believe. You could be the greatest living Aquinas scholar or the most brilliant Van Tillian presuppositionalist, and the bugman is trained to deny the reality you show him. Showing the bugman how scripture clearly corresponds to reality will do nothing. Reality does not matter to him. He denies reality itself. Reality is whatever he wants it to be. He is willing to submit to the idea that 350-pound lingerie models are beautiful, that men can become women, that police across America are hunting black men for sport, that sodomy is a perfectly fine basis for social order, that wearing a cloth mask is a greater act of moral courage than giving your life for your country, that having children is selfish, and that the 2020 election was the most secure election in world history. With someone like this, for whom reality is totally inverted, how on earth do you think you will persuade them of anything?

Throughout the history of the church for nearly two thousand years, the job of the Christian apologist was to demonstrate how the truths of scripture and the Christian religion correspond with reality. But the job of the Christian apologist in current age is very different. He must first demonstrate that the world you live in is *not* reality, and awaken you to the world as it actually is, and to *then* show you how the truths of scripture and the Christian religion correspond to the real world that has been hidden from you for your entire life.

Therefore, the globohomo cinematic universe that the modern bugman lives in must be chopped down. All of it is a seamless garment. Trannies, open borders, acceptance and promotion of sodomy and other sexual perversion, feminism, abortion and antinatalism, anti-white race hate (so-called Critical Race Theory), pornography, and the entire consumerist lifestyle are a single Donar's Oak that must be sent through a woodchipper.

The bugman takes pride in being irreligious, but he is not—this is the religion of the modern bugman, the modern Canaanite. There is a time for patient, reasoned argument, but the bugman needs to see his shrines get chopped down while his gods are totally impotent to do anything about it. The need of the hour is to teach especially Christians to hate the fake and gay globohomo cinematic universe. You must despise it. You must learn to reject it for the fakery that it is. It is a world that is not real. It is a world *designed* to make you reject the faith of your fathers. It is a world designed to make you an Esau, selling your birthright for a mess of pottage.

In order to wage warfare and fight for the kingdom of God, he must learn to hate all that which he has been browbeaten into showing indifference to. The globohomo, liberal consumerist order is not something we can simply agree to be neutral about. We have to hate it. Whatever good things may have existed in these institutions in the past have been cordycepted—in that, there is nothing left but a zombified, animated corpse. Learning to hate the consumerist fake reality that has been foisted upon us places you back in reality. You no longer are a slave to whatever the current thing is, led around by your baser impulses, but are once again someone rooted in tradition that extends far beyond yourself or the current day. Your very existence is a thing that demonstrates the impotence of the globohomo gods. No matter how many hundreds of billions are spent by the propaganda machine or academia and scientism industry, they are powerless to capture your heart and your soul. All their mighty, seemingly miraculous powers are for naught.

Your very existence is a shattered oak to the bugman.

CHAPTER 2
Economic Emasculation

But if anyone does not provide for his own, and especially for those of his household, he has denied the faith and is worse than an unbeliever.

1 TIMOTHY 5:8

The uncanny valley of Admiral "Rachel" Levine and NCAA women's swimming "champion" "Lia" Thomas is just too much. The pot has been turned up just a bit too high and the frog jumps out. But what they do not realize and what is most crucial for them to understand that the tranny is the *endpoint* of a rebellion against the created order that has been waged since well before they were born. Blurring the flesh and blood distinction between men and women is the culmination of spiritually confusing men and women *for generations*.

Yes, feminism has been around for a very long time, much longer than most realize in fact, but it did not gain widespread acceptance until the economic and social structure of western society began to change. For all of recorded human history in virtually every culture in every part of the planet, men and women, mothers and fathers, husbands and wives were implicitly understood to be totally distinct. Men are not women and women are not men. But it was not until the modern economy reached a point in industrialization that the characteristics that make men biologically distinct from women began to be nullified by technology that what had been totally distinct now started to become interchangeable.

Utopian social engineers throughout the eons would have loved what only became possible in the twentieth century. Major economic activity in the past required physical strength and dexterity. Plowing fields, sailing ships, building structures, protecting (and plundering) goods, etc. all required the strength of men. This is not to say women in the pre-modern world were not industrious, but rather that their economic activity was within the context of the household. To put it crassly, their most significant economic contribution was the production and nurturing of subsequent generations, but it was obviously not their only contribution. Food, clothing, and household goods were all manufactured by the skillful hands of ancient and premodern women, almost always within the context of the household. There were no ancient basketweaving factories or a manufacturing center full of looms. There were households. Husband and wife, mother and father, both worked in tandem. This might seem like historical trivia to many, but it was basic human experience for nearly every person born on this planet until about the twentieth century.

The Social Engineers' Blank Check

It was not until industrialism reached its zenith that the labor men and women could provide was no longer distinct. Women had been brought into factories in England and the United States since the earliest days of industrialization; the household economic activity they had performed since time immemorial had moved into the cities at scale, but even then *married* women in these factories was not extremely common until the twentieth century. In the industrial revolution's nascent days, the most dangerous industrial work was still performed by men. It was not until industrialization became so advanced that it merely required a mere human being pressing buttons and pulling levers, and the industrial economy became so advanced and productive that most economic activity was no longer centered around physical production. The economic lines between men and women, that had existed for all of human history in every place, became totally blurred. In other words, we produced so much stuff so easily that now the majority of work centered managing and facilitating consumption. Most of the labor a modern post-industrial economy demands does not require the strength of men; consequently, from an economic perspective, men and women are interchangeable.

But the problem is, despite the economic circumstances changing, despite rapid advances in technology allowing us to produce what even the most affluent of our ancestors would deem utterly absurd wealth with incredible ease, men and women are still distinct. Men and women are not the same. Technology may have narrowed the raw economic utility gap between men and women, but men remain biologically, emotionally, sociologically, spiritually, metaphysically distinct from women. And after two or three generations of a modern, post-industrial economy "liberating" women from the duties of motherhood and the household, the chickens have come home to roost. There is a direct line from Rosie the Riveter to a pink-haired, septum-pierced, androgynous orc teaching your preschooler about anal sex.

Industrialization made inclusion of women into the labor force possible, but not inevitable. It took a global, industrialized war making both the traditional source of labor—men—scarce and the widespread inclusion of women into the labor force socially permissible through necessity. It was not lost on the financial and corporate interests in the postwar era that they could double the size of the labor force, increase productivity, and bid down labor costs by making what seemed like temporary wartime measures a permanent feature of society.

The prosperity of the postwar era, when America was the only industrial power on the planet that hadn't seen its industrial base destroyed by warfare, gave the United States an economic advantage over the rest of the planet, and created opportunity for wealth that average people had never had access to before. Demand for labor was massive. America was the factory for the entire planet. For the average American family, the calculus was simple. "The kids are in school, I am at home bored, why not earn extra income so we can buy a cabin upstate, go on vacation, and pay for the kids to go to college? What would be the harm?" But the result has not been households remaining intact and with a little extra income; no, the household has been dismantled and its "human resources" have been auctioned off to the highest bidder. And the social changes that have resulted in the two or three generations since are massive. Every sociological statistic signaling cultural destruction has risen exponentially in this period. Divorce, out-of-wedlock birth, decline in marriage rates, decline in birthrates, single-parent homes, etc. have all skyrocketed as the traditional household was broken up.

But it is not as though our grandparents and great-grandparents were aware of the bargain they were making. Greater prosperity for your individual family was within reach, the consequences of this dramatic change across all of society were difficult to foresee.

But eventually, rather than families being formed first, and then moms going to work, a woman's economic and sociological *telos*—her primary purpose to both the economy and society—became her career. Therefore, for subsequent generations, the economic and sociological *telos* of woman was indistinguishable from men. Have a career and make money became the primary driver of the economic existence of man and woman together. Doing the thing that God formed your kind to uniquely do, produce and nurture new human beings, became a merely optional function of feminine existence.

For all of human history anywhere on the planet until that advent of liberal, democratic, postindustrial consumerist society, if you asked a little girl what she wanted to be when she grew up, she might look at you with bewilderment at such an anachronistic question. What was there to be but the glorious and noble privilege of wifedom and motherhood? But today if you ask a young girl what she wants to be when she grows up, a shrinking minority will say "be a mommy" while the rest will have answers often no different than all the little boys. The liberated feminist beams with pride at such things, but what is the young woman liberated *to?* A nihilistic existence slaving at a cubicle, filling a spreadsheet, sending emails, for *other* men, men who do not love her, nor care about her beyond her economic utility. A life of a few hours of free time a week, spent consuming, sometimes meals and drinks at Instagrammable cafes and bars, other-times bingeing on insipid Netflix inanity. They are liberated to soulless existence, an existence of consuming product until you cease to exist. They are liberated from the burden of meaningful, purposeful existence; a womb is not the place future generations are produced, nor are breasts the appendages where future generations are nurtured, no, they are junk no more useful than the appendix that can be chopped off and stitched up.

The Ancient Slave Woman and the Liberated Modern Woman

The "liberation" of feminism is the liberation for a woman to willingly embrace the life of an ancient slave woman. Consider the very earliest passage of *The Illiad*, when the priest of Apollo, Chryses, pleads with Agamemnon to give him back his captured daughter, Chriseis:

> The king dismissed the priest with a brutal order ringing in his ears: "Never again, old man, let me catch sight of you by the hollow ships! Not loitering now, not slinking back tomorrow. The staff and the wreaths of god will never save you then. The girl— I won't give up the girl. Long before that, old age will overtake her in *my h*ouse, in Argos, far from her fatherland, slaving back and forth at the loom, forced to share my bed! Now go, don't tempt my wrath—and you may depart alive."[1]

1. Homer, *The Iliad*, trans. Robert Fagles (New Yord: Penguin Books, 1990), 113–114.

The life that Chryses was desperate to prevent for his daughter, to be uprooted from her home and from all those who love her, to toil away pointlessly for the benefit of someone else's household, to have meaningless, empty sex with someone who does not love her, on and on until she dries up and is discarded, this is the life that feminism has sold to women with the paper-thin veneer of consent—since you freely chose the life that was the greatest fear of ancient women it therefore must be an unqualified good! But that is what the life of the liberated woman is, the life of the ancient slave, packaged in the language of liberation and freedom. But this "liberation" is nothing more than the destruction of the fundamental way of life for all of humanity—the household.

The destruction of the household, the tearing apart of the fabric of human existence for all of history, is the root of the anti-human ideology that has resulted in transgenderism. You cannot have your cake and eat it, too. You accept the economic interchangeability of men and women while rejecting the supposed biological interchangeability of them. It is baked into the cake.

This is not to say women within a household should never produce income. Women producing income has been common throughout history. But this was always—until Trashworld—something subordinate to the duties, obligations, and responsibilities within the household. The point of existence for the woman is not to work and then consume product, any more than the point of the man's existence is to work to be able to consume product. A man works, and builds wealth to marry and establish a household, a woman marries and produces and nurtures the next generation for her family and her nation. If you were to say that sentence to any one of your ancestors before the twentieth century, they would stare at you blankly, wondering why such an obvious thing would need to be said. If you say such a thing out loud in current year, you will be despised by all who hear it. When you criticize this fake and gay transhumanist reality most people live in, you should expect to be hated.

Reducing both to genderless economic nodes in a global economy has done wonders for GDP and the growth of Fortune 500 corporations, but it has been disastrous for society as a whole and the souls of individual men and women. The entire structure of the economic system is built to emasculate man, to reduce him from being conqueror of empires, tamer of untouched wilderness, builder of cities, and father of households and nations to being a replaceable wage slave in a cubicle under the thumb of HR harridans. This modern economic system, that destroys the household, that reduces men to geldings, that turns mothers into slaves to faceless corporate oligarchs must be destroyed. You must learn to despise it like so much else in Trashworld. Once you do, you will realize the consumable delights, the entertainments, the toys and other schlock of this monstrosity you live in are not worth the cost—the selling of yourself and your offspring to Mammon. And when you refuse to pay that cost, your very existence is an ax to the root of this hideous and fake reality.

Escape From Trashworld

I remember the day I realized I was living in Trashworld. I once took my wife on a date to a restaurant in a hip retail and entertainment development in an affluent suburb of a large American city. Full of trendy bars and restaurants and complete with tiny, absurdly overpriced studio apartments above them. The place was filled with twenty- and thirty-somethings clad in Patagonia sweater-vests, women carrying Dolce & Gabbana handbags, each enjoying one of the three dozen IPAs on tap and extremely expensive appetizers with finely diced fresh herbs sprinkled upon them (a premium you pay so you know they did not come out of a microwave or deep-fryer). You could overhear conversations about Marvel movies or *Game of Thrones* or *Girls* or whatever the pop culture Current Thing happened to be. The food tasted fine, but it was not memorable. What I did remember about that place was that there was not a single child anywhere. Not only not at that particular restaurant, but anywhere in that entire development. The place was designed specifically for childless people. It was designed to be a place women take that night's Bumble date. It was designed for a spiritually homosexual people, for whom life is a matter of consuming fleeting pleasures before you expire, to get those fleeting pleasures. I do not remember the taste of that food, but I will never forget how overcome I was with melancholy upon the realization that this place, this lifestyle could only be achieved when built upon a mountain of tens of millions of dead babies. That is what must be understood by the Christian in the current age: the lifestyle that is idealized and glamorized and highly sought after by all—the cosmopolitan, independent, urbane, hip, affluent young person free from all responsibility—is one you must learn to hate. That is the end to which the murder of children, the abandonment of all sexual mores, and the destruction of the household is dedicated: so that you can live on Pleasure Island without ever turning into a donkey. That is what the pro-life movement consistently fails to recognize, the end to which the murder of babies is sought. People murder their offspring because they want to enjoy this fake and gay world, but in order for Christendom to return, it is a world that you must learn to hate. The "nice things" we are desperate to enjoy are the chains that keep us trapped in this world, and you must learn to associate them with everything you are fighting against. *Sex in the City* brunch-life must be put to sword and fire, this will only come if you first put it to death in your own heart.

Only when we begin to say no to the enticements of Trashworld and instead despise them with a passionate rage will the fake reality come crashing down.

CHAPTER 3
Atomized Man

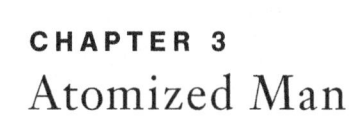

My God, My God, why have You forsaken Me?
Why are You so far from helping Me,
And from the words of My groaning?
O My God, I cry in the daytime, but You do not hear;
And in the night season, and am not silent.

PSALM 22:1-2

If everywhere you go, you know, even subconsciously there is nobody on this planet who would give their life so that you might live, how psychologically devastating would this be to an individual? Now imagine an entire society where this is the case for a significant percentage of the population. Would it not look exactly like ours?

Nothing characterizes the dystopia of our modern, liberal consumerist society more than the profound loneliness, isolation, and alienation experienced by young men and women. It is extremely common for young men (and even young women) to have no friends they regularly see in person. This epidemic of loneliness has been a topic of discussion in academic circle's since the publication of sociologist Robert Putnam's *Bowling Alone* (2000), but it's time that Christians learned this lesson. It is not possible to understand the spiritual miasma of our era without recognizing how extraordinarily lonely most people are.

Many young people have very few friends they can interact with in-person on a regular basis. The enthusiastic embrace of lockdowns in 2020 showed just how used to isolation people are. A typical day in the life of the young man in the modern world is to wake up, leave home, sit in a car for part of an hour, arrive at work, interact with people from whom your existence is nothing more than a means to a paycheck[1]. He drives home alone in his car for part of an hour. Even the brutalist architecture that surrounds him is designed to make him feel alone, to feel as though he is as plastic and disposable as the environment in which he lives. He goes home, alone, maybe to interact with virtual friends on social media or video games,

1. If you think this is overly cynical, consider that everyone who has ever changed jobs after working at a place for a long time will know just how circumstantial most work friendships often are. Most people are conscious of how transitory relationships at work can be and therefore never become meaningfully close with anyone.

maybe to consume entertainment and pornography alone. He is isolated. He is distant from his family, a family that has been fractured since his parents split up when he was very young. This physical, emotional, and spiritual distance imposed upon him will define his relationships for the rest of his life. The few friends he made in high school and college have all gone their separate ways. Some have married and live seemingly happy lives. Others are just like him. Loneliness overwhelms him like the waters of a flood coming up around his neck. Every waking second of his life he is confronted with the fact that no one really cares whether he exists or not.

This may seem hyperbolic. It may seem like an exaggeration. But these are the conditions that many young people live in today. No one really knows them. No one really cares about them. They have been abandoned. Forsaken by everyone that should care. When horrible things happen to you, you must face it alone. You lose your job and there is no one to comfort you. You get diagnosed with cancer, and there is no one to console you. You die, and there is no one to mourn you. Your existence is totally meaningless and every part of you that has not yet been numbed feels unrelenting pain.

A Factory for the Production of Human Misery
We have manufactured a society that maximizes human despair. The most distressing thing about the vile, distorted reality that has been forced upon us is the intense

emotional and spiritual suffering it produces. Our modern Trashworld is a factory for the production of torment and misery. You must understand that it is an industrial packing facility for *garmonbozia*, the tangible form of human suffering (and food for demons) in David Lynch's *Twin Peaks*. In fact, if Satan were to design a society where every lust and every sinful desire could be freely pursued, and men would then feel the maximum possible misery, how much different from our society would it look?

We have never had more widespread access to comforts the kings and emperors that ruled our ancestors could not have even dreamed of. Even the poorest people among us have their food preserved by a magical contraption that keeps it cool. They can communicate instantly to anyone on the planet at any time with a tiny device in their hand. For a day or two's labor they can board a small, metal, mobile building that magically transports them through the air to any place on the planet. When once daily meat consumption was reserved for kings, our homeless beggars have never gone a day without the ability to eat a cheeseburger.

And yet, since we are born into it (and any understanding of history has been actively suppressed) we have absolutely no perspective to appreciate the hysterically absurd prosperity all around us. For all of human history, in every place on the globe, there was no greater cause of death and disease than hunger and starvation. However, in our world, the greatest threat to the heath of the poor is obesity-related disease. We have more abundance than any people in the history of the planet, yet we have never been more miserable. We are totally awash in despair. There has never been more depression, anxiety, mind-altering SSRI use[2], illegal drug use, drug overdoses, and suicide than there is today. Think about the comparison to our current standard of living to the past. Think of all the times when suffering and death were an ever-present specter haunting every moment of each man's existence—the innumerable periods of war, famine, and disease, such as when the Black Death was killing one third of the population of Europe in the thirteenth century. Are we any happier today than these men? If anything, despite living in widespread material conditions as close to a utopian state as any time in human history, we are the most depressed, anxious, and tormented people who have ever lived. We have been all but liberated from material constraints yet have never been more miserable.

Why is there so much despair? Why is seemingly everyone medicated with psychotropic drugs? Why are we surrounded by the telltale SSRI stare? Why is there an epidemic of opiate addiction and overdose death today? Why do so many prefer death to existence in this world? Whether they can articulate it or not, all the things that make life worth living have been torn away from them. They have no meaningful relationships. They have no

2. SSRIs, or selective serotonin reputable inhibitors, are commonly prescribed antidepressant medications, including Zoloft, Paxil, and Prozac.

place to belong. They have no people to belong to. They have no fathers or brothers. They are totally and absolutely alone, even as they are surrounded by millions of others. God did not create man to be alone.

As it turns out, that verse in Genesis[3] is not *only* about marriage and sexual reproduction. It is also about man's need for others more generally. God calls the feeling of loneliness "not good." Literally everything else in the creation *was* good. But not man's condition of loneliness. Trashworld seeks to make this the normative condition of man. Man has been alienated from family by divorce, bastardy, chaotic and broken homes, and emotionally, physically, and sexually abusive family. He has been conditioned to never develop friendships with other men; never put himself in a position to trust anyone else. With women, he is incapable of true intimacy because even the instrument that secures a relationship between man and woman in permanency—marriage—has been eaten away like a maggot-gnawed corpse. To that end, every step in the process toward marriage has been likewise putrefied.

Trashworld has eaten away everything within the order God has created that gives stability to human relationships. Just as the relationship between husband and wife has been destroyed by divorce, fornication, and neglect, so has the sacred relationship between father and son. We have a nation of bastards, as Michael Foster

---

3. Genesis 2:18.

has pointed out.[4] My own experience as a man teaching and coaching in public schools confirms the same. Within thirty minutes, I can spot with 100 percent accuracy which boys in the class or on the team are being raised by single mothers. They will flagrantly misbehave to get attention, then, after you chew them out, they will sidle up to you like a little puppy dog. They have no idea, but they are craving the attention of men. They are desperate for surrogate fathers to love them, to discipline them, and just have a man they respect care about them. Millions of young men go their entire childhood without anything like this. And the consequences of this for our entire society are palpable.

Similarly, the strong bonds of friendship among men, that very thing that both builds cities and also conquers them, has been made lurid and an object of derision. Close male friendships with intense expressions of love, like Frodo and Sam, David and Jonathan, Alexander and Hephaestion, or Abraham Lincoln and Joshua Speed, are assumed by the porn-addled brains of bugmen to *of course* be homosexual. It is not just because the bugman is hypersexualized and cannot fathom any kind of love but the erotic; it is also because they have never experienced anything like love from another man. They are like men who only drink from a fetid swamp encountering fresh, spring water. This is why they attack it. They must not let anyone experience the strong bonds of brotherhood

---

4. Michael Foster and D. Bnonn Tennant, *It's Good to be a Man: A Handbook for Godly Masculinity* (Moscow, ID: Canon Press, 2022), 107ff.

among men, because to do so would begin to disassemble this factory of despair.

Atomization as a Means of Political Control

All of this goes much deeper than making life miserable for individuals. It is an intentional instrument of social and political control. This is because close relationships between men, where deep bonds of love and loyalty are forged are *essential* to life. They are the basis for the polis and, therefore, for politics. The polis is not a random collection of individuals living in close proximity. It is a people, a body politic, united by a network of friendships sustaining it. You cannot have a community of human beings living together without men who love their neighbors enough to die for them. "Greater love hath no man than this, that a man lay down his life for his friends" are the Lord's words from John's Gospel (15:13, KJV). If you go your entire life never having had a friendship with someone who is willing to die for you, have you ever even experienced love? Imagine an entire people like that. A nation is, among other things, a group of people connected by love. What would it look like for these bonds to be totally broken?

We live in an anti-polis, something that increasingly looks like a collection of millions of random and anonymous individuals, not one single individual with a relationship with others beyond what is necessary for bare economic utility. Would not a place like this be awash with anguish, depression, anxiety, mental illness, drug use, suicide, and other deaths of despair? Men are not created to be alone, but to love and to be loved. Trashworld is designed to rob men of love, even the common grace of love that non-Christian societies have enjoyed since time immemorial—even the wicked Cainite civilization of Nod. What our overlords have begun to create and envision for all of us is a society that is subhuman, one where meaningful human relationships have been abolished.

It may seem like tin-foil hat territory to say this has happened by design. No, there are no leaked documents from the World Economic Forum or Trilateral Commission or Davos outlining the plan to make all of humanity alone and miserable. Nevertheless, it is reasonable to conclude that things have not happened by accident. Reducing human beings to atomized individuals is a means to produce an astonishing level of political and social control. In a post-industrial information age, where data is king, our overlords want us so isolated and alienated that we would be easier to rule via a social credit algorithm.

When a man rules slaves, he wants every slave living only for himself. He doesn't want slaves to have families and true friendships. He doesn't want slaves to be loved and to love. He doesn't want his slaves to have something and someone worth killing for and dying for. He wants each individual slave to be totally committed to his slave's own personal self-preservation above all else. The perfect slave is the lonely narcissist who believes everything you want him to, yet thinks his slavery is freedom and his credulity is free-thinking. The perfect slave wears his chains as though they are tokens of his freedom.

It is within this socially engineered world of atomized, isolated individualism you dwell. It is *designed* for you to feel alone and powerless. This is a feature not a bug. I often end up in discussions on politics with well-meaning conservative men from the baby boomer generation where someone will bring up the latest leftwing abomination and we agree that things are getting really bad. It is always at this point that the well-meaning Boomer will say, "Well, if things get bad enough, we still have the guns."

Leaving aside the fact that we have reached the point where borderline personality disorder moms castrating their little boys for attention is a thing that has entered the mainstream, I don't know how much worse it would get to reach "if things get bad enough" territory. There is nowhere near the kind of social cohesion in America to do anything about it when things get bad enough.

If the governor issues a gun confiscation executive order, and the state patrol SWAT team is on its way to your house, and you are going to resist this confiscation violently, who are you going to call to come to your aid? Who is going to risk death or life in prison to preserve your Second Amendment rights? Which numbers in your contact list are you going to call? Who would actually show up to help you versus SWAT? This idea persists among the generation that has living memory of the kind of social cohesion that existed when America was still a functioning country, but that world is dead and buried.

The story of the Battle of Athens, Tennessee, is well-known and widely celebrated in right-leaning corners of the internet. Shortly after the Second World War, GIs returned home to a rigged local election and used their recently gained combat skills to successfully lead a violent revolt against their corrupt municipal leaders. The kind of high social trust, high social capital that existed in America in that generation is something that no longer exists.

That kind of thing could never happen today under our current social conditions. This is the reason they have not tried to confiscate firearms in the United States like they did in Australia and other countries. They don't need to. If you hand every slave a rifle it will make him *feel* more free while simultaneously allowing you more control over him—and both of you know it will never be used. Firearms in America act as an ice cube the frog will cling to as the pot continues to boil hotter and hotter.

The average person who believes "If it gets bad enough we still have the guns" has almost no one who would fight and kill and die for them. Yet they seriously think the silent majority of the country would take to the hills to fight a brutal, grueling, decades-long guerrilla war like the characters from *Red Dawn*. If mutilating the genitals of children isn't enough to motivate the conservative masses into violent revolt, *nothing* is going to cause that. Many who believe conservatives will one day be pushed to violently revolt point to the recent defeat of the most powerful military in the world in Afghanistan. Yes, it is indeed remarkable that illiterate peasants in isolated Himalayan valleys defeated the most technologically advanced fighting force the world has ever seen. Trillions of dollars were spent on the invasion and occupation of Afghanistan, yet the goat herders were victorious. The example of a guerrilla army such as the Taliban defeating the U.S. military breathes life into the "If it gets bad enough, we still have all the guns" cope. Comparing the social conditions in the United States to that of Afghanistan, a premodern society where the same people have lived in the same isolated villages for millennia, where tribal loyalties and blood feuds dominate, and where there is an inexhaustible wealth of social capital, is absurd on its face. These are people who have been fighting—while massively outnumbered—against powerful empires for hundreds of years. They have each undergone privations for an entire lifetime that the average American could not bear for an afternoon.

America was like this at its founding. It was even like this into the nineteenth and twentieth centuries. The same social cohesion, the same martial spirit, the same love of neighbor and family and nation that led small militias to victory against the most powerful, most advanced, most well-supplied military force in the history of the world in the colonial era, propelled America through its expansion, its own internal warfare, and the creation of a nascent military and commercial empire. But all of this has been eaten away in a few short generations. No one has family to fight for. No one has friends and neighbors to defend. Their nation is but a mere ephemeral idea. Now, everyone is alone, isolated, atomized. For the bugman, no one is coming to defend him, and he has no one to fight for.

The loneliness and atomization of modern man are necessities for Trashworld to exist. They, too, are a part of the oak that must be cut down. They are a necessity for it to exist, but at the same time they are also a vulnerability to it. Young men are now far more aware of their own isolation, and desperate to seek out community. This engineered loneliness becomes a vulnerability when it allows for the formation of new communities of men formed out of opposition to those who rule us. Men may be conditioned to be atomized and isolated, but they are not *created to* be that way, nor do they desire it. Men desire community. Men desire to belong. Men desire friendship. Men desire a tribe. If you restore true camaraderie among men, you are picking up the ax to chop down the idols of this age.

CHAPTER 4
Biological Castration
Engineering Modern Androgynous Man

"*Nor let the eunuch say,
'Here I am, a dry tree.'*"
ISAIAH 56:3

God has made men to be men. To be distinct from women. To have testosterone and defined musculature. Yet the average twenty-two-year-old man today has the same testosterone levels that the average, Social Security-eligible man had a little over twenty years ago. No, that is not a typo. Young men today have less testosterone than elderly men had in previous generations. We are not like the men of a generation ago, much less the heroes of old.

It is good for young men to think of the heroes of the Bible, classical antiquity, and the Middle Ages, the great warriors like David, Odysseus, or Roland, and want to be like them. The strength and vitality these men had is incomparable, even when compared to the greatest men of the modern world. In single combat, David would effortlessly add a trophy of Jocko Willink to the dowry bag. Odysseus would easily best LeBron in any athletic contest, including putting an inflated calf skin through an iron hoop, and Roland could crush Thor Bjornsson's skull with one bare hand while breaking his thousand-pound deadlift record with the other. Our greatest men are nothing compared to even the ordinary men of the past, much less the great warriors who have not been forgotten to history.

But we are nothing like even the ordinary men of antiquity. We do not have the same spirit. It has become something of a cliche to compare Millennials and Zoomers to the men who landed on Utah Beach, but the reason it is done so often is because it is so obviously true. We are nothing like those men. The environment that birthed them is a relic of history. Just as the Ancient Near Eastern civilizations collapsed in the Bronze Age or as Rome collapsed as the medieval world dawned and everything about them, their art, their culture, their technological advances simply were lost, so too is the world that shaped and formed the men who were our great grandfathers. We still have roads and bridges and infrastructure of that world—for now, but the most obvious tell that you are living in the ruins of a once great civilization is that where we once had men, today we are now left with androgynous, obese bipeds with (optional) male genitalia.

All you have to do to see this in the most vivid way you can, is to compare what people look like today to your parents' or grandparents' wedding photos. The fattest person in those ruffled tuxedoes or bridesmaid dresses with puffy sleeves would look emaciated by comparison today. You also see this when watching footage of people on the street or on the beach from fifty years ago. Everyone had normal BMIs. Obesity, much less morbid obesity, was extremely rare. Why is this the case? Why are we so fat? And why do we keep getting fatter?

A Food Supply Made of Industrial Waste
Like so much else that is corrupted in Trashworld where all that is true, good, and beautiful is inverted and reality is totally distorted, the very sustenance that comes out of the earth to give us life has been turned into poison. It is a simulacrum of food rather than food itself. It is damaging your body, mind, and soul. The distorters of reality have actively worked to make the entire society believe industrial byproducts are desirable and good for you. We have already seen how every social more that grounded us in reality, that maintained social order, that made family formation possible and therefore kept civilization alive, was stripped bare by

the intense propaganda of a massive academic, journalist, and entertainment complex. And while all that took place, in a completely different sphere of the human experience, the medical, pharmaceutical, and agricultural complex inverted the reality of human nutrition. This is no coincidence. No sooner than the plague of no-fault divorce, abortion, and feminism began to be visited upon us that a plague of obesity and androgyny appeared as well. They demonized the nutritional wisdom filtered through millennia of trial and error in favor of technocratic, scientistic superstition—and the result has been the eradication of men.[1]

The environment we live in has been designed to emasculate men. Not just the social and cultural environment, which is self-evidently true, but nearly everything we eat, drink, breathe, and touch has been tainted, made to make you fat and program your hormones to emasculate you. This is something that many people, even those aware of many of the other destructive features of Trashworld sometimes have a hard time with. It is hard to be told that the food you eat, the food you *like*, is poisoning you. If you feed a child cereal his entire life with a few drops of Clorox in the milk for his cereal, he would naturally treat such a thing as normal. He would expect to have bleach-flavored milk and he would react

1. Whether the financialized and industrialized food supply's emasculation of men is by design or accident, I will leave to the reader, but it is worth pondering that one of the very few industrial food additives that has been banned as "toxic" in the United States is borax, which is found to boost testosterone levels.

angrily if you told him that it is making him sick. Imagine, now, the overwhelming majority of the food everyone eats (and loves to eat) is like this.

It is a great tragedy that when the truly horrid Michelle Obama attempted to barely tweak public school lunches (keeping the same industrial slop but topping it with a few leaves of kale), conservatives reacted by now double-fisting Big Gulps to wash down even more soon-to-be-diarrhea from Burger King. You are what you eat. If your food makes you obese and slovenly, depletes your testosterone, saps you of all vitality, and turns you into a fat, androgynous goblin, you will get angry when someone points this out.

Many well-meaning Christians will say, "But the ability to have such abundant sources of food, unlike any other time in the history of the world, has to be seen as a blessing. We should give thanks for this." But you can have such a liberal definition of what constitutes food that you can almost become a kind of gnostic denier of reality. If someone told you they had communion with some Triscuits and a sugar-free Red Bull, you would rightly rebuke them. But if someone says their diet of paint thinner, corn syrup, and reconstituted animal byproducts is food, we treat this statement as sacrosanct.

This conservative reaction is understandable, in some ways, because, much like concern for the environment, the mainstream right has totally abandoned the issue to the left. If you say you care about the environment, this means you believe the world will be destroyed by climate change by 2030 and we must pass the Green New Steal. The only other option is fertilizing your lawn with diesel fuel and burning a mountain of tires in your back yard to own the libs. Of course you can care about the forests, lakes, and streams, and the animals that live in them and be on the right. In fact, lack of concern about them is fundamentally left wing.

It is the left that is characterized by its rejection of both material and metaphysical reality. Mainstream environmentalism is steeped in this rejection. How else could it be mainstream in trash world otherwise? Multi-billion-dollar corporations strip-mine third world countries to build batteries for Teslas and amass undecomposable fiberglass windmill parts to make their astroturfed climate Greta of Arc stop shrieking. But they could not care less about how much they have destroyed human, animal, and plant life, so long as "big line go up" and keep going up.

It is the same way for food. Many conservatives will act as though your only two options are either being a granola-crunching, quinoa-devouring, white person in dreads and Birkenstocks, *or* a four-hundred-pound human slug with Mountain Dew on an IV drip, absolutely sedentary if not for motorized carts. You can avoid becoming the latter without becoming a crunchy, granola lib. There are other options. But the other options must be conscious. If you take the path of least resistance, you will end up a doughy, androgynous humanoid like so many others. You must consciously choose a path of difficulty to simply have what has been considered normal physique for most of human history.

Manufactured Food for a Manufactured Reality

If we can feed the entire world, but that "food," while providing sustenance to keep life going, turns men into creatures less than men, can we truly call it food? We have to admit that the tremendous efficiency of modern, industrial society in producing high agricultural yields as well as almost totally eliminating waste in the processing and distribution of food, comes with tradeoffs. And at a certain point, the tradeoffs are simply not worth it, both to the individual and society he lives in. What good is it to feed the whole world, yet lose your soul? What good is it to never be in want of food, but be transformed into a creature that would be unrecognizable to any of your ancestors? Central to Trashworld is a sort-of gnostic denial of the fixed, created order. There are no real distinctions between men and women, men can even become women and vice-versa, and industrial sludge is blessed sustenance from the hand of Almighty God. Should we be thankful that at least we are not starving? Of course. But we should not take the poisoned, estrogenic swamp we are stewed in as something it is not. The atomization of society is a feature and not a bug. While we should be thankful that we have digital friends from social media and the encouragement they are to us and how they keep us from going insane, we cannot and must not pretend they are a substitute for real, flesh and blood relationships with other human beings. Similarly globalist food, while it will keep you from starvation, it is likewise no substitute for the plants and animals God created for us to thrive.

Five percent of Americans under the age of thirty describe themselves as transgender.[2] The trans contagion is just a finishing of the castration the environment and food supply has started. To escape this grotesque world you have to summon the will to not follow the path of least resistance. Simply going with the flow and doing what everyone else does will make you a fat, sick near gelding. You have to actively choose to do the opposite of so many of the things which are considered normal. You must understand, like so much else, you have been lied to about what is healthy. The serpent lied to our first parents, telling them they would not die if they ate from the tree of knowledge of good and evil. The demons that animate this monstrosity we inhabit are lying to you in much the same way. And when you discover that you have been lied to about this, and you begin to take the difficult steps to return to a more human-scaled way of life, a way of life in line with how God created the world and your body, mind, and soul will begin to feel masculine once again. And men with the fire of virility

2. Anna Brown, "About 5% of young adults in the U.S. say their gender is different from their sex assigned at birth," Pew Research Center, June 7, 2022, https://www.pewresearch.org/short-reads/2022/06/07/about-5-of-young-adults-in-the-u-s-say-their-gender-is-different-from-their-sex-assigned-at-birth.

once again rousing them will naturally undo much of the devastation of this pathetic world. It must begin with the changes you make today.

CHAPTER 5

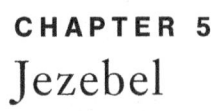

Jezebel

The Woman Formed from the Bugman's Rib

> *Nevertheless I have a few things against you, because you allow that woman Jezebel, who calls herself a prophetess, to teach and seduce My servants to commit sexual immorality and eat things sacrificed to idols.*
>
> REVELATION 2:20

The disgusting world of filth in which we live is designed to make its inhabitants unable to define the distinction between men and women. No one has any idea what a woman is. No one has any idea what a woman is uniquely created for. Like so much else, this is not an accident; this is not random. People with cultural, economic, and political power have designed things to be this way. This all had been a long, deliberate process moving toward its ultimate end. We began with all cultures everywhere, throughout all of human history implicitly recognizing the unique strengths, weaknesses, and the distinct roles and gifts that belong separately to men and women. We have arrived at "Rachel" Levine, "Lia" Thomas, and "Caitlyn" Jenner.

Transgenderism as the Apotheosis of Feminism
For most people in our culture today, just the thought of there being things that women cannot do that men can, and vice-versa, seems no different than doctors draining the body of bad humors with leeches. They say "The modern world has bridged the gap of the differences between men and women. In fact, our medical technology is so advanced that we can even bridge the *biological* gap between the sexes." Our modern, transhumanist world believes it has so effectively cast down the Almighty and has triumphed over His created order so decisively, that His very image, man and woman, this thing that He has fixed from the very beginning is now permanently abolished.

But as much as modern man deludes himself into believing he has killed God and set himself upon His throne, he has hilariously fallen short. Shaving down the cartilage in a man's Adam's apple, giving him silicone breast implants and female hormones, and removing his genitals and replacing them with a rotting, putrefied, permanently open wound—which is only possible with antibiotics that already have rapidly diminishing returns—does not transform a man into a woman. It only creates a horribly disfigured man. It is putting a man in a dress and makeup, and stuffing a brassiere with tissues, but with several extra and *irreversible* steps. Modern man has not conquered God's created order. He has not even conquered Uncanny Valley.

Nevertheless, the blurring of the line between man and woman that comes to full bloom in transgenderism had its beginnings centuries before we had the ability to do so with the surgeon's scalpel. The sexual revolution began at around the same time *all t*he revolutions got their start, back when men wore frilled shirts and pantaloons, and women wore corsets. At the very outset of the Enlightenment, when men first believed they had bested God, did the earliest feminists begin to spread their ideas. As the Jacobins were putting the political and social order at the heart of Christendom into blender, people like Mary Wollstonecraft (1797–1851) were doing the same to the sexual order that God made on the sixth day of creation. The demand that women and men are fundamentally the same had its roots this far back. Like all the other monstrosities of the modern age, feminism had been there in seed form centuries ago, waiting for technological advances to fulfill the grand, utopian designs they had only theorized after casting the Triune God from His heavenly throne. This horrible, revolting

Trashworld is the way it is because people have decided to design it this way. What we currently live in is the product of generations imagining they can re-create the world in our own sinful image. Transforming the glories of the woman into the shameful things of the man is not an accident. It was done by design.

Revolutionary Utopianism

When we think of the sexual revolution, we think of free love in the sixties, the introduction of birth control and legalization of abortion. All leading to the rapid increase in promiscuity in the generations to follow. But this is the deluge that comes after a dam has collapsed. The undermining of that dam began much, much earlier. Feminism in America began its attack on the household as the fundamental unit of society in the early nineteenth century. Concurrent with the feminization of American Christianity in the aftermath of the Second Great Awakening, the earliest feminists in the United States believed that the women civilized the men, and thus it stands to reason that they should therefore have the same political and legal rights as men. The household was an antiquated notion for a barbaric age, and women were to be at the forefront of a new and better, more enlightened society. While they were far less violently revolutionary (and vastly less sexually permissive) than the European feminist contemporaries, the American WASP feminists were no less utopian. They believed they could transform the rowdy, alcohol-fueled independence of the American frontier into an ideal society by banning demon rum. The utopian social engineering of temperance was not just about banning alcohol, either. The goal was to take away the important political organizing center of the tavern from their main political foes—the urban, high church Lutheran and Catholic immigrants whom they also wished to civilize. The point of it all was a revolutionary re-ordering of society.

Regardless of the particular historical circumstances, whether it is in revolutionary Europe, early industrial America, or technological, globalist society, feminism has *always* been a utopian ideal. However, it has always been dystopian in practice because it is in direct rebellion against the way God has created man: but from the beginning of the creation, God made them male and female (Gen. 1:27). Any and all boundaries that God has made immutable are the object of the idolator's fury. This is true of all the idols of this pathetic age, but most of all the idol of feminism. You are born what you are and had no choice in the matter. They can conspire together to attempt to restructure our entire way of life to make the definition of man and definition of woman seem less and less distinct, but every, single cell in your body cries out that you are *one thing* and not *the other*.

But this is the fundamental deceit of this repugnant age: we believe that we are so much better than ancient men, but the truth is we are less different than we think. The idolatries of the ancient world and modern age are the same in that they both seek to invoke the power of their demon gods to transgress the immutable boundaries God has set. Compare a pagan to the denizen of Trashworld. Imagine a Germanic woman offering her firstborn to Odin for a good harvest and houseful of children. Compare this to a twenty-first century American woman offering her firstborn to Mammon so she can keep sending emails all day between Bumble dates and margaritas. The only difference between the two is that the latter gives up her soul for far less in return. They will do heinous, unspeakable things because they cannot bear the fact that God has made the world the way that He has made it; He has set us within impassable mountains and the deceitful gods promise a way over them. That is the nature of the world whose shrines Boniface chopped down, and that is the nature of the current repellant age.

The woman of this disgusting Trashworld has been stripped bare of all those things which God has given her that make her glorious. You must understand *that* is what feminism is. It is not making men and women equal, for that would be like making gorillas and horses equal. They are two different things! Feminism has done to women spiritually what female-to-male transgenderism has done to women physically. Feminism sought to make women and men the same in every way apart from the physical and biological. Transgenderism gruesomely completes that final step. A woman is given hormones so that her smooth, beautiful face begins to have the patchy beard of a barely pubescent boy. Her breasts, those bodily organs that provide sustenance to her offspring and whose beauty attract a mate, are chopped off. Her uterus and vagina, the womb and door to life, are cut out and sewn shut. A piece of flesh from her arm is sewn onto the place her genitals were and fashioned into a limp, dead, totally impotent, and nonfunctioning member. The transman *is* the physical embodiment of what the feminist is spiritually. The glory of woman is removed, and she becomes a pathetic, miserable imitation of a man.

Suffrage Is Warfare

This was what those who opposed the first-wave feminists of the Progressive Era—the anti-suffragettes—understood[1]. Politics is war by other means. And voting is a proxy for civil war; rather than lining up your side versus the other side and shooting at each other, instead we agree to count how many are on each side and agree to peaceably respect the results of the mock battle. The women who *opposed* giving women suffrage understood that giving the woman the right to vote was spiritually the same thing as asking her to pick up a rifle and go to war. These woman clearly had political interests, just as they would have a very keen interest in a war their

1. A good example of this is this anti-suffragette article from *The Atlantic* (yes, **that** *The Atlantic*) by Lyman Abbott, "Why Women Do Not Wish the Suffrage" from September 1903: https://www.theatlantic.com/magazine/archive/1903/09/why-women-do-not-wish-the-suffrage/306616.

husbands went off to fight. But they understood that politics is a man's duty to his household just as it is his duty to fight in a war that threatens his wife and children. Politics is a proxy for warfare. The famous dictum of Clausewitz "war is politics by other means" is just as true in the inverse. There is a built-in hierarchy of duties and responsibilities that God has established for mankind. The pro-suffrage egalitarian idea of liberalism rejected any hierarchy, even (especially?) hierarchies established by God Himself. It held not having the right to vote made a person less human and imbued with less moral worth than those who did. It also did violence to the tradition of republican government within English common law, which premised that only those with the most to gain or lose, the landed gentry, should have the right to vote. The same standard was adopted in America's earliest days. Not all men had an equal say in government; only those who had skin in the game, those with land, would have a say in who would rule. It is true that law affects both rich and poor, greater and lesser alike, and throughout history landed men have had a responsibility to their people and a sense of *noblesse oblige*. And when this is destroyed, a society ceases to function. Egalitarianism flattened the distinctions between men, removing the principle of skin in the game from the body politic. Egalitarianism destroyed the concept of the household as the fundamental unit within society. The economic, cultural, and social atomization of man, as discussed in the previous chapter, was preceded long before by political atomization. He was dethroned as head of his household; now his vote could be canceled out, and the proxy civil war that is democracy now was free to invade the peace of his hearth and home.

The first wave feminist, as their anti-suffragette contemporaries well knew, had conscripted women to political warfare. God had told Israel in Deuteronomy 22:5 that it was an abomination to Yahweh for women to put on literal armor, vessels, or implements of a man.[2] There is a direct line from the first wave feminists introducing women into the proxy war of democratic politics to the most destructive perversions of Trashworld in Current Year. Yet nearly everyone, even ostensible conservatives, shrieks in horror at the mere suggestion that perhaps the Nineteenth Amendment might have caused some problems.

So thoroughly has the radical egalitarianism of liberalism infected us all that we, without giving it any thought, agree with them that moral worth comes from participation in electoral politics. We just presuppose it without consideration. Never do we ask, "If this is so fundamental to what is true, good, and beautiful, why did nearly all societies everywhere for all of human history mostly exclude women from politics? Why was there such intense

2. And no, sorry feminists, Deborah, in Judges, did not put on armor and start throwing Canaanites around like Xena: Warrior Princess or Wonder Woman. A close reading of the text (Judges 5–6) shows that Barak went down from Mount Tabor to lead the troops into battle (as God had specifically commanded him to do) while Deborah remained on the mountain. The entire description of the battle was with him in command and leading troops and Deborah providing moral and spiritual support.

opposition to women's suffrage? Are the feminists right that it is because until we became enlightened in the most horrific, barbaric, destructive, and deadly century in human history, all men everywhere were utterly misogynistic and believed women should be reduced to nothing more than breeding stock? Or did our ancestors understand something about the way God created the world? Did most of them, believing that God created man and woman to live together in order and peace in the most healthy, prosperous arrangement possible, understood this through cultural osmosis even though they might not have been able to articulate it? Could it be that these truths, which everyone once implicitly understood, had to be violently beaten out of them by a program of social engineering? Did such a program deconstruct the imperfect but very good way of life that they once had? Was it implemented to rip away from them and their children the economical and cultural wealth their ancestors had toiled to build and to reduce them to anxious, nihilistic, and hopeless consumers?

Conservative Idolatry

The Nineteenth Amendment isn't going away. That toothpaste is not likely to go back inside the tube. Even hinting at the suggestion that it should be reversed will have you officially labeled a disturber of the peace. And that should tell you something: Even exploring why anyone in the past might have had a rational cause to be against it is verboten. The closer you get to a people's idols, the more extreme the fury you will provoke. Even those who purport to be on your side will despise you. But if you are going to fell the impotent idols of this detestable, putrid age of filth, you are going to have to ask uncomfortable questions about topics that *everyone* thinks of as unqualified, universal goods. You will need the faint-hearted, conflict-averse *conservatives* who are ostensibly on your side to say yes when asked, "If the only way to prevent the mainstreaming of gender mutilation of kindergarten children were to go back and prevent the enactment of the Nineteenth Amendment, would you do it?" I have often been in conversations where questions like this were raised and have observed that much force is needed to get conservatives to see that the idols that they rightly detest are downstream from the idols they are comfortable with.

The most difficult challenge in felling idols among a people is not even in the chopping down but in exposing the idols as idols. The conservative wants this much blurring of the distinction between men and women *and no further*. The progressive in twenty years will advance from optional gender reassignment surgery to mandatory, while the conservatives will accuse Democrats of being the *real* transphobes. To quote Michael Malice's riff on R.L. Dabney, "Conservatism is progressivism driving the speed limit." At the time I am writing this, the purportedly ultra-conservative Fox News employs the former Bruce Jenner as a paid commentator. To be the iconoclast you desperately need to become, you need to ask not, "What if we dropped from 55 mph down to 35?" but, "Why can't we turn the car around and floor it?" If you are not asking questions that will outrage *conservatives* from time to time, even if you think you are a radical, you are actually going the speed limit . . . and still going the wrong way. And the idolatry of feminism is one of the main shrines at the heart of the globohomo pantheon, and you are still driving on the road it paved.

If they can repress the natural and even biological desires of women, if they can keep the beach ball under the water for as long as they can, they will be able to keep all of society atomized and isolated. Without mothers, as opposed to "birthing individuals," you do not have a civilization. Without mothers nurturing their children, no families, no households can exist. Women, not men, were given wombs to carry children. Women, not men, were given breasts to feed children. Women were designed to be the anchor of their households and the bringers and nurturers of life. One must do violence to the glorious image of God that they bear in order to make them wombless, breastless, pathetic and miserable imitations of men. Until we are willing to admit that feminism, even (especially!) the feminism accepted by conservatives, is a demon goddess responsible for our enslavement, we will remain under the shade of the oaken shrines of Trashworld. You must summon the courage to confront and tear down these idols, or you will ever remain a slave.

CHAPTER 6
Bugmen in the Cocoon
Education in Trashworld

Luxury is not fitting for a fool,
Much less for a slave to rule over princes.
PROVERBS 19:10 (AUTHOR'S TRANSLATION)

In 100 years we have gone from teaching Latin and Greek in High School to teaching Remedial English in college.
JOSEPH SOBRAN

There is no better aphorism than "You don't know what you don't know" to describe the condition of learning in this idolatrous and repugnant age. No one has any idea just how much of the massive wealth of their heritage they have had hidden from them. It is as if you are the sole minor heir to a multi-billionaire, and custodians of this almost unquantifiable wealth have never so much as alluded to these riches while you live in a crack house and subsist on ramen, never knowing that every wall and crevice around you is stuffed with hundred-dollar bills. You have access to astonishing wealth, yet you live in abject poverty. No civilization has dedicated more wealth and time to education as ours has, yet we are vastly more ignorant than our ancestors of even two or three generations ago.

How Far We Have Fallen

If you look at the standards for getting accepted to a university 150 years ago, you will see the precipitous decline. In 1869, Harvard University's entrance exam[1] contained questions testing the breadth of knowledge of applicants to the university with questions such as these:

> Describe the route of the Ten Thousand [from Xenophon's *Anabasis*].
>
> [Describe the battles of] Pharsalia, Philippi, Actium,—geographically and historically.
>
> [Give brief biographies of] Leonidas, Pausanias, Lysander.

1. View the whole exam at https://static01.nyt.com/packages/pdf/education/harvardexam.pdf.

Prove the values of the cosine of 0°, 90°, 180°, 270°.

Prove that the perpendicular from the centre of a circle upon a chord bisects the chord and the arc subtended by the chord.

On top of this, applicants were required to make translations from Latin and Greek to English and vice versa. Keep in mind, these are the questions meant to sample the education of teenagers *entering* university. Today, you almost certainly will not be able to find a *graduate* of Harvard University who could answer more than one question correctly from each section of the test, much less be considered worthy of gaining access to their alma mater 153 years ago. Words cannot describe the decline in what passes for educated among the elite in the intervening years. Those being trained to rule the planet do not even have what our great–great-grandfathers would consider a sixth-grade education.

Ta-Nehisi Coates, a former columnist for The Atlantic, one of the great public intellectuals of the current day, and a recipient of MacArthur Foundation Genius Grant, admitted he had never heard of St. Augustine.[2] Another top public intellectual from Current Year and fellow MacArthur Genius Grant recipient, Ibram X. Kendi, who is the nation's leading expert on racism, is unable to define that word without using a tautology. The academy

---

2. Ta-Nehisi Coates, "My Heroes. Your Stamps." *The Atlantic*, December 27, 2012, https://www.theatlantic.com/personal/archive/2012/12/my-heroes-your-stamps/266672.

is hopelessly overrun with "research" papers on things diversity, equity, and inclusion as it pertains to any subject, rather than actual scientific or historical research. When someone says they have a PhD with a dissertation on scientific research you expect to see a paper on something like noncommutative quantum field theory, but instead her dissertation is on "Gendered barriers to Australian Antarctic research and remote fieldwork."[3] Since Stanford professor John Ioannidis published "Why Most Published Research Findings Are False" in 2005[4], which showed that the majority of medical research papers cannot be replicated, the scientific world has been thrown into something called the Replication Crisis. What Ioannidis demonstrated is that research is accepted not on the basis of scientific method, but rather whether it is peer reviewed and cited incestuously elsewhere in academia. If Ioannidis's findings are correct, a substantial amount of published research can be presumed to be fraudulent— in other words, our scientific institutions are one, giant, Ponzi scheme. There are billions spent on education and research and almost nothing to show for it. The "science" the bugman worships is quite literally a false god, in more than one sense.

3. Meredith Nash, et. al., "'Antarctica just has this hero factor . . .': Gendered barriers to Australian Antarctic research and remote fieldwork," *PLOS*, January 16, 2019, https://doi.org/10.1371/journal.pone.0209983.
4. John P.A. Ioannidis, "Why Most Published Research Findings Are False," *PLOS*, August 30, 2005, https://doi.org/10.1371/journal.pmed.0020124.

But it is not just education at the very top, i.e., elite universities training the next rulers of the world, but academia as a whole. The entire education system is incapable of producing an educated populace. Despite spending hundreds of billions of dollars every year on education, more than half of American adults are unable to read proficiently.[5] If there *were* a secret conspiracy to loot the populace, make them believe they are the most, well-educated people who have ever lived, while in reality they have been made one of the stupidest of all peoples to have ever walked the earth, how would it look any different than this?

Manufactured Ignorance

Throughout all the history of all mankind in every civilization everywhere, if you held slaves, the *very last* thing you would do would be to give them an education. You would not want them capable of thinking for themselves. You would never want to give them the tools where they could challenge your domination of them. From ancient Greece and Rome to the Antebellum South, it was illegal to teach slaves to read.[6] The reason is obvious: You would not want to encourage a slave revolt.

5. Michael T. Nietzel, "Low Literacy Levels Among U.S. Adults Could Be Costing The Economy $2.2 Trillion A Year," *Forbes*, September 9, 2020, https://www.forbes.com/sites/michaeltnietzel/2020/09/09/low-literacy-levels-among-us-adults-could-be-costing-the-economy-22-trillion-a-year.
6. Yes, there are examples of household slaves in the ancient world who were indeed well-educated and even served as tutors, but for every one of these there were thousands worked to death in mines and fields.

We must grasp that this age of refuse and filth is, in many of the ways that matter, very little different from the ancient and pre-modern world. And our system is also little different. We believe because modern, liberal, egalitarian society abolished the formal institutions of slavery that slavery qua slavery has been eradicated. But it very clearly has not. Instead, it is wrapped in a thin veneer of consent. If you were a wicked, evil social engineer and were going to design a massive slave state, the very best conditions would be where the masses believed they were totally free and that their own bondage was their choice. The most valuable slave is the one who believes that, because he chose these chains, and not *those* shackles, he is free. His very chains would be cherished emblems of his freedom, and if you attempt to remove them, he reacts violently. What slave master wouldn't want slaves like that?

The education system in Trashworld is designed to produce the perfect kind of slave. You have been taught to read but also not to value this skill. You are left totally ignorant of the great literature and tradition that formed the civilization whose ruins you walk through. Math and science are intensely taught like an aboriginal cargo cult painstaking building a runway and weaving wicker airplanes in the hopes free stuff will appear. All of it gives the pretense of education. We spent the billions. We spent the years in the classroom. We have the degrees. But it is all nothing but a skin suit. It gives the illusion of education without actually being educated. And that, more than anything else, is the entire point.

I first came to this realization when I attended a convocation at a small, Christian liberal arts college. An address was read by the history professor, and in passing he stated something to the effect that if you had not read Herodotus you cannot consider yourself a historian. I had just graduated with a bachelor's degree in history from a large public university, and I was fortunate to have merely *heard of* Herodotus. My unfamiliarity with real history, with actual primary documents from the tradition that undergirded everything, had been totally withheld from me. Even nearly twenty years ago, my college history classes were on topics such as class struggle among medieval European peasantry and women's rights in colonial America. I knew less about history than someone with a sixth grade education a century ago, yet I have an official credential showing I know history. I was totally ignorant, yet I had paid tens of thousands of dollars to be told I was well educated, and I am not an outlier.

What you must understand if you are to combat this world of mass human subjugation is that most people do not want to be told they are slaves. They have been programmed to believe they are free. You will not be able to convince them what they perceive as freedom are actually chains. What you must instead do is give yourself and those within your sphere of influence the actual education that has been stolen from you. If you do this, if you are liberated from your ignorance of the history and tradition of the world that shaped your civilization and your ancestors, you will bring even the greatest experts and public intellectuals of this decrepit age to utter shame. Even their best and brightest are very stupid people. A plumber who has read *The Iliad* or *City of God* is better educated than most of the PhDs now living. By simply learning the great many things that have been hidden and obscured, you will cast down the idols of Trashworld.

PART TWO

Transforming the Felled Trees of Trashworld into a New Christendom

CHAPTER 7
The Bedrock for a New Christendom
Worship That Grounds Man Back in Reality

> *Therefore, since we are receiving a kingdom which cannot be shaken, let us have grace, by which we may serve God acceptably with reverence and godly fear. For our God is a consuming fire.*
>
> HEBREWS 12:28-29

The modern world is an atomizing, global slave state. It has torn you away from all that God created you to hold dear—your God, your family, your friends, your kinsmen, and your nation. It is designed to transform you into a mere individual concerned only with survival and consuming away your own boredom. So often, young men reach out to me, disenchanted with Trashworld, desperate for something more, asking how to make their own lives better, and my instinct immediately is to say, "Go to church." Unfortunately, I'm forced to hesitate.

Why? Because the modern, conservative evangelical church has failed to oppose this globohomo Trashworld in any meaningful way. We have not even been a speedbump to the onslaught. There are a multitude of reasons for this. If you want to begin to understand the failures of the evangelical church in America, it didn't start in the 1980s with the Moral Majority or with fundamentalism in the mid-twentieth Century. If you want to know why it feels like America is circling the toilet bowl today, the place you must begin looking is the Second Great Awakening.

The Decline of American Christianity
Before the 1820s and '30s, Christianity in America looked more or less like it did in Protestant Europe in the centuries that followed the Reformation. But as the country began to expand westward on the frontier, new religious phenomenon began to occur. Along with the development of cults such as Mormonism and what would become Adventism, revivalism began to take over what had been standard, theologically orthodox Protestantism. Men like Charles G. Finney would hold tent revivals with dazzling oratory and salesmanship to generate religious excitement and manipulate the emotions of the crowd to produce "conversions." Variations of this

method eventually became the baseline for evangelical Christianity in America. Thanks to men like Charles Finney, the church's worship became fundamentally about evangelism, and no amount of crass spectacles, emotional manipulation, or crafting the church's worship to fit the fancies of the unbelieving world can ever be too much. If you talk to any of the most devout evangelical Christians you know, and you ask them what the church's worship on the Lord's Day is about, they will tell you it is primarily for reaching the lost or presenting the gospel. When the leaders of evangelical churches get together to determine how worship on the Lord's Day should look, Marketing and Production reign supreme. While The question of how God tells us He wants us to worship Him is seldom considered. If it is brought up, the immediate retort is, "Well, the New Testament doesn't say very much about worship, so we have freedom to be led by the Spirit." While it seems to be true that no specific liturgical practice is detailed in the New Testament, the answer to that question betrays a semi-Marcionite view of Scripture. Because we treat the first two-thirds of the Bible as historical appendices, we miss all that the Bible has to offer about worship.

How Then Should We Worship?

The *entire* Bible has much to say about what worship is and how it should be done. Contrary to popular evangelical opinion, it doesn't become nullified and made totally irrelevant by Christ's birth, death, resurrection, and ascension, but is rather fulfilled in it.

From the very beginning of Genesis, the place where man encountered the presence of God to worship was the Garden. After Adam was expelled from God's presence in the garden sanctuary, men would draw as near to God as they could. They could come up to the gate of the garden, which was guarded by a cherub with a flaming sword. We see Cain and Abel doing just this in Genesis 4, offering their worship to God. From that point on, we can see that worship is about drawing near to God's special presence on earth. Noah, Abraham, and the other patriarchs constructed altars to do just this, to draw near to God's presence to worship Him.

God matured humanity and established newer and better covenants with His people, giving them greater authority, giving them greater promises and covenant signs. He also refined and developed how His people would draw near to Him in worship. He gave them a sacrificial system in nascent form in Noah, then a detailed process of drawing near under Moses and Aaron complete with a mobile, replacement Garden of Eden, the tabernacle.[1]

Later, under David and Solomon respectively, a sacrifice of song was added to the liturgy, and a new, permanent Garden of Eden, the temple, was constructed.

---

1. For a more detailed discussion of the biblical development of worship see Jeffrey J. Meyers, *The Lord's Service: The Grace of Covenant Renewal Worship* (Moscow, ID: Canon Press, 2003).

God's people would draw near to Him, have their sins forgiven, be consecrated to Him, offer their tithes and incense and prayers to Him, share a meal with their God, and be blessed by Him and sent out.[2] If we were ignorant of what the Old Testament tells us about worship, we would easily fall into the false idea that since the New Testament doesn't seem to say anything about worship, worship is just a grab bag to do whatever we like—fertile ground for pragmatic, consumerist, post-Second Great Awakening evangelicalism.

The reality is that in the New Covenant the big things that have changed is that *blood* sacrifice is fulfilled by the death and resurrection of Jesus Christ. With the coming of the Spirit at Pentecost, His people become the living stones of a new temple and wherever they gather to worship *is* the temple—the New Garden of Eden where the presence of the Living God dwells on earth.

Rather than throwing out what the Old Testament says about worship, the New Testament unlocks it. The process of drawing near to the presence of the Triune God, has now been opened up to all His people, Jew and Gentile, not just in Jerusalem but throughout all the earth. Rather than Leviticus being a boring book where every Bible-in-one-year plan goes to die, the sin offering, the ascension offering, the tribute and incense

---

2. The process for the Mosaic liturgy is laid out in Leviticus 9. Its correspondence to God's pattern of covenant making in Scripture and our worship in the New Covenant is explained in detail by Jeffrey J. Meyers in *The Lord's Service*.

offering, and the peace offering have deep meaning for the Christian on this side of the resurrection and Pentecost. These meanings are made clear in weekly worship. In fact, before the Second Great Awakening, traditional liturgies throughout all of the church in all the world—Eastern, Western, Catholic, and Protestant—followed a more or less similar pattern and structure as the Hebrews followed when they drew near in Leviticus. Our ancestors did not mindlessly follow some dead tradition of men before revivalistic evangelicalism sprang up in the 1820s and '30s, allowing us now to have Hillsong music, smoke machines, and laser lights.

The reality is modern worship is just as divorced from God's order as anything else in globohomo Trashworld. If liberal, consumerist society is defined by an individualism that reduces all of life to products to be consumed, American evangelical worship is absolutely a part of this system.

If "going to church" is simply another product crafted for them to consume, no different than a movie on Disney+ or a burger at Shake Shack, they might still encounter Jesus Christ if the Word of God is preached even a little bit, but they will be just as vulnerable to the Donar's Oak of the globohomo cinematic universe as they were before. Perhaps they will be even more vulnerable than before. Since they have heard some of God's Word, but its power has been denied, they will become like a man whose demons were exorcized by the Pharisees in Matthew 12:43–45. The outcast fiend returns with seven more demons, and the last state is worse than before.

Against Consumerist Christianity

Worship that is in line with consumerist individualism will fail God's people and lead them to worship themselves. Throughout Scripture, worship is absolutely central to the life of God's people. Over and over again, when they forsake worship of Yahweh for that of foreign gods, all of society falls apart. It then becomes oppressed by foreign occupiers, and life remains terrible until the people repent and call upon the name of Yahweh, worshiping faithfully once again. If the way the church worships is fundamentally about what *you* want, the thing that is being worshiped is not God but you. Traditional liturgy guards against this because the way God's people draw near to Him is not crafted by marketers to get the most butts in seats, but rather by long-dead fathers in the faith who collectively meditated upon God's instructions to us.

So much of the antipathy toward traditional Christian views of worship betray the same modern hubris that marks everything in our decrepit age. We willfully throw out the inheritance of wisdom gathered by generations of our ancestors. As the late thinker Roger Scruton said, "In discussing tradition, we are not discussing arbitrary rules and conventions. We are discussing answers that have been discovered to enduring questions. These answers are tacit, shared, embodied in social practices and inarticulate expectations."[3] Scruton is speaking of

---

3. Roger Scruton, *How to Be a Conservative* (London, UK: Bloomsbury Continuum, 2019), 21.

tradition more generally, but his words are obviously applicable to traditional Christian practice.

It is very true that traditional liturgy is not a panacea and can also be treated as just another product to be marketed and consumed. Quite often all things "trad" are merely another consumerist expression. This has happened increasingly as disenchantment with the fakeness and atomization of the modern world that people feel, yet cannot articulate, and finds its expression in a craving for "authenticity."

Having the most authentic product to consume becomes yet another iteration of the thing people were reacting to in the first place, i.e., churches market their traditional liturgy as a way to return to authenticity over and against big box megachurch rock concert worship. This is akin to eschewing cheap, plastic, mass-produced garbage from Walmart for expensive, seemingly handcrafted, mass-produced garbage from Bespoke Post. Following a traditional liturgy must first and foremost be done to obey God and pursue worship to please Him. And in doing so from that standpoint is a thing that forms and shapes men who are impervious to the parasitic modern world.

Churches that believe the entire Bible and draw near to God to honor Him, that do not fear to sing His war songs from the Psalter and new songs shaped by them, and that keep the feast and regularly celebrate His body and blood are often rare. Most faithful, conservative Christians who have grown increasingly disenchanted with this Trashworld, and who are desperate for something, anything! like this nearby them simply do not have it. Many would have to drive an hour or more one-way each week to find something like it.

If you recognize how central worship is to society, to your family, and to you as an individual, your options are very limited. If you no longer want to keep worshiping at a place where worship is a commodity and where the music and preaching are crafted to shill Jesus to consumers, you can either move to a place where worship is done faithfully, OR you can work to establish a church founded to worship faithfully where you are. Either option involves pain, sacrifice, and a lot of work. But such work is necessary.

The Wuhan flu pandemic revealed the decline that has existed for a long time. The decline had been easily hidden by the appearance of material affluence, but is now everywhere in society, and the church is no different. Like Israel in the Old Testament, we have replaced worship of Yahweh for different gods, but instead of Baal and Asherah, the gods we worship in contemporary evangelicalism are ourselves. Just like Israel, we must forsake these gods by returning to worship in a way that is not crafted to entertain our fickle attention span and tickle our ears, but one that we have not chosen as a product to consume, but a holy duty to fulfill. And just like Israel, when God's people forsake worshiping their false gods, God raises up deliverers for them. This is the pattern that repeatedly takes place throughout the

Book of Judges. God's people worship false gods. God would send foreign armies to occupy and oppress them. The oppression would get so bad that the people finally repented of their idolatry and worship Him rightly. And in response to their repentance, He would raise up deliverers like Ehud, Gideon, or Jephthah. Everything that happened, in all of society, ultimately was the result of either faithful or unfaithful worship.

Worship is the engine that drives everything. All the fakeness and gayness of the liberal consumerist order flows directly from the church worshiping the whims and feelings of men. The foundation of a new Christendom must come from rejecting this totally and instead shaping our worship upon what God says in His Word.

You have to understand that this battle is *not* a materialistic one. In fighting the idols of this age, you are not fighting against flesh and blood, you are fighting against principalities and powers, against the rulers of this age, against the dark hosts in the heavenly places. You don't fight such a war at the ballot box or even with rifles and tanks. You fight it by drawing near to the presence of God on the Lord's Day offering yourself as a living sacrifice cut up by the priestly two-edged sword of His Word and burned up by the fire of His Spirit. You are doing battle against the demons that animate this hideous dystopia you live in. That is how you have to understand worship. You are drawing near to the Triune God this Trashworld is at war with. He is feeding you from His Word and at His Table, and God and His people are dropping fifty-megaton bombs on the gates of Hades. You are chopping down the shrines of demons and building Christendom out of the lumber.

CHAPTER 8
Masculine Economics
Restoring Father as Provider

A good man leaves an inheritance to his children's children,
But the wealth of the sinner is stored up for the righteous.

PROVERBS 13:22

Closely related to reestablishing worship, which strikes at the heart of global memeplex fake reality, is the restoration of the household as the ultimate mode of human existence. Fundamental to this is restoring fathers as the providers and protectors of a household, rather than income earner one of two. The father must be head of his household, and he has to be able to provide for his wife and children for it to exist as a *household* rather than a home with two hired servants that outsource the household functions to other hired servants. Few want to grapple with this important distinction.

What Is a Household?

Perhaps you are unsure of what model has been missing, and so I must first help to explain what a household is.[1] It is not merely two married people and any children they may have living under one roof. A household is a micro-nation. A household, like individual men and individual women, has a distinct *telos*. It exists for a purpose, to pursue a particular goal. Unlike the nuclear-family arrangement of the postwar era, it does not exist merely to perpetuate existence. Producing and raising up future generations is *one* function of the household, but it is not the *only* function of it. Our first parents were told to fill the earth *and s*ubdue it. The household is the basic unit of conquest.

But of those today who actually do get married, the purpose of their union rarely is so purposeful. It is often an instrument of greater consumption for consumption's sake. Even children are treated as consumer goods, a mere lifestyle choice, rather than the very purpose that

---

1. I am indebted to C. R. Wiley and Allan C. Carlson for much of my understanding of the household, which comes from their respective books *The Household and the War for the Cosmos* (Moscow, ID: Canon Press, 2019) and *The Natural Family* (Milton Park, Oxon, UK: Routledge Press, 2017).

God created marriage for. Within such an arrangement, you do not have husbands and wives nor fathers and mothers; you have instead income earner one and income earner two. The purpose is to pool two incomes together to have access to greater and nicer products to consume. A palatial house. A sexier car. Exotic vacations. More stuff for the 1.7[2] cute, little human pets you have chosen to keep. These are not households in the sense that anyone who has ever lived until the twentieth century would understand them. They are not households. They are economic co-prosperity zones.

To reestablish the household is a task that is simultaneously of massive importance and monumental difficulty. Everything in modern life is set up to make having a household next to impossible. The structure of marriage laws. The artificial scarcity of housing and other destructive economic chicanery. A society that has violently rejected distinctions between men and women. To consciously choose to reestablish the household is to swim not against a tide but against a tsunami. Nevertheless, to do so and do so well is a direct, public challenge to the fake and gay Trashworld that it cannot answer: "Why would you intentionally build a household full of future men and women being trained to conquer the

---

2. The total fertility rate per woman in the United States is, at this writing, 1.784 live births per woman, well below the 2.1 required to sustain the population. See "U.S. Fertility Rate 1950–2023," Macrotrends, https://www.macrotrends.net/countries/USA/united-states/fertility-rate, accessed July 6, 2023.

world, when you can have a vasectomy at twenty-two and an entire room filled with Funko Pops?!"

You might say, "Well, just make a lot of money and the problem will solve itself." It is hardly that simple. The wealthiest men on the planet—Jeff Bezos, Elon Musk, Bill Gates—do not have (and have never truly had) households. Wealth on its own does not create the conditions for this. You and your wife must intentionally take this path to become a household, not merely a family. The modern family, with its labor capacity auctioned off to the highest bidder, has more in common with ancient slavery than it does the household: You can be married. You can even have children. But you are owned by a master. Sure, your master treats you well, and your wife's master treats her well. You receive lavish amenities. You have a nice McMansion in a safe cul-de-sac away from crime. You might even get to own a BMW or a brand-new F-150. You get to enjoy plentiful food and drink. You get to wear stylish clothing. Your respective masters even give you free time every so often to take your children (who are raised by strangers while you serve your masters) to places like Disney World. You might even be able to choose to leave one master for another. But you will always have a master.

We don't think of this existence as slavish because we equate slavery with utter destitution and barbaric, torturous abuse. But in the ancient world, that was not universally the case. Some slaves were indeed worked to death in mines. Others lived decent, full lives tending to fields and herds. And others lived comfortable lives in the households of nobles. But one thing was certain—slaves did not have their own households. We think modern life is not the life of a slave because of comparative luxury, but the *structure* of modern life is almost the same. In fact, ancient slaves with wives and children had something much closer to a true household than modern men today, especially the intentionally childfree.

The life of freemen and nobles, however, existed in the context of households. While a household was not autarkic, it had a high degree of economic independence. It was led by a father, with a mother wielding authority and supporting the household's mission. Children were raised within the household, being brought up to inherit households of their own from their fathers and grandfathers. And the end of these households was directed to was the upbringing of the next generation and to take dominion of the creation.

When you think of the purpose of the traditional household within that frame, the modern family arrangement of our fake consumerist reality, where it is a pooling of resources to consume more and children are a mere lifestyle choice, only differing from purchasing a dog by a matter of degrees rather than kind, you begin to see how absurd it all is.

The entire force of a multibillion-dollar media and entertainment propaganda regime has been employed for generations to psyops men and women into despising the things God has designed them to love. God designed men to love their wives and their children and to desire so intensely to have a wife and sons and daughters that he would kill and die for them. Generations of psychological and social conditioning has diverted the course of this great river of passion to flow instead to cheap consumer goods, vapid entertainment, and pornography. The deep passion has been turned inward to create innumerable legions of narcissists. A similar thing has happened to women, the fury of a mother whose child is threatened has also been turned inward and directed against the object she was designed to protect—her child—if that child threatens access to brunch. The womb, the very place of comfort, protection, and safety, has been turned into a slaughterhouse. The thing God has created us to love and protect has been turned into an object of hatred, because powerful forces have manipulated the lusts of the masses.

Instead, you must reject these deceitful passions. You were not created to enjoy all the pleasures that are possible in a six-by-eight cell. You were not created to be a bug in a hive, responding to stimuli until you expire. You were created to fill the earth and subdue it. You were created not to be a bug in a hive, but a free man conquering, subduing, and filling unowned space. God created man to take dominion of His creation (Gen. 1:28). The fake world you live in is constructed to subvert this impulse or to redirect it. You can conquer unowned virtual space in an open-world video game or the Metaverse, but the flesh and blood world is already owned, so don't bother.

But this is a world to be conquered, and the means God has given you to subdue the earth is the household.

The Economic Devastation of Trashworld

Trashworld has been engineered to make having a household extremely difficult, but this is something for you to overcome, a dragon that God has given you to slay. In previous generations it was not anything that anyone even had to think much about. If you took a wife, you had a household. Everyone implicitly understood what that meant. No one had to read a book about marriage and households. You just assumed it as if by osmosis. But today things are different. Everything is set up to oppose the formation of a household, even if you are consciously desiring to have one.

As was said above, the entire economic system is set up with the assumption of dual incomes. They have intentionally made providing for a household on a single income extremely difficult. They want households with moms staying with the children to be an upper-middle class luxury lifestyle, totally inaccessible to the majority of the population in the middle and working class. Median incomes have declined, particularly for men, while housing and healthcare have consistently increased. For the generation just starting out today, things are far more difficult. The boomer might well be right that the millennial and zoomer just doesn't have the work ethic his generation has, but he does not consider how much greater that work ethic was rewarded in his day (and how disincentivized it is today). Things are quite a bit harder than they were in 1975. This did not happen by accident. The people who rule our society have chosen to create these conditions.

But there is a difference between acknowledging how much more difficult life is now for young men and dejectedly acquiescing to defeat. Many who point out how much worse it is for young men than it was for their fathers and grandfathers (who are largely oblivious to the way things are) conclude that they should just give up and not even try. This is folly. Just because the mountain you must climb is steeper does not mean it cannot be conquered. You must give up pretensions that you will have a life as comfortable as the boomers enjoyed, but a good life where you can support your wife and your children is attainable if you carefully plan for it. You need a vocation that matches both your abilities and interests. There is never-ending debate about whether or not young men should go to college. Obviously, universities provide nothing close to the education they did even a generation ago, much less when those institutions were founded. And slightly less obvious is the fact that the system is very clearly engineered to funnel everyone with an IQ high enough to write their own name into a four-year university and a lifetime of debt slavery. The system is insidious.

Conservative stuffed suits will loudly proclaim how you should "Just pick yourself up by your own bootstraps" and decry the idea of student debt forgiveness. Some rightly understand the politics, recognizing such a thing is a subsidy for our enemies; knowing that many degree holders are merely the foot soldiers of wokeness. But what they do not see is that a system that deceives gullible teenagers into a lifetime of debt by promising them a nice middle-class life is abominable and highly destructive to the fabric of society. The destruction of the social fabric is the means to opening the door to further unthinkable insanities even beyond child genital mutilation.

There are many, many people who are pushed into going to college that should never have gone. Many who should have been plumbers, mechanics, HVAC specialists, etc., and would have earned a large enough income to provide for a household, but instead took on massive, non-dischargeable debt to be trapped in barely-above-entry-level white-collar jobs, making just enough money to be an enjoyer of all the trivialities of modern consumerism, but not nearly enough to provide for a household. Millions have fallen into this trap. Very few fathers and pastors had the foresight and courage to tell them to avoid it. Who wants to tell a young man that he is not bright enough for college? Particularly when the reality distortion machine has beaten the message that college is the only path to a good life, and the college—and student loan processor—are more than happy to let him in.

If you are a young man reading this, trying to decide what you will do with your life, you need to take an earnest appraisal of yourself. If the year were 1960, would

I be going to college? Am I far enough on the right side of the IQ bell curve to pursue a degree in a difficult field like engineering or computer science? Or will I be going for a layup like communications or sociology? If you are just going to college because that's just what you are supposed to do, you should not go. It would be better to pursue a trade, which has lower ceiling but a higher floor, than to subject yourself to poverty indefinitely.

Despite the risks, both economic and spiritual, of attending university, upper middle class vocations should not be abandoned. We will need men who should be doctors, lawyers, accountants, salesmen, engineers, etc. to do such vocations and do them well. Men who *can* do such things and would enjoy doing them *should* pursue such vocations. We have to be honest about what we are. The globalist, consumerist pseudo-reality has imposed a ridiculous egalitarianism upon our society—most people believe that with enough time, effort, and money spent on education *anyone* can become *anything*. In reality, however, this is not the case. God has made some men to be plumbers and roofers and warehouse workers. He has made other men to be CEOs and software engineers. There is dignity in all work, especially work being done with the intention to support a household.

The egalitarianism of Trashworld is rooted in a despising of the working class. They hate the idea that rough men build their homes, drill the oil that powers their lives, drive the trucks that keep their existence going. They would rather be impoverished, white-collar wage slaves than part of the great unwashed. You must be painfully honest with yourself about what you are. Your enemies want you to share their hatred of the working class, and they want you to be a bug in a hive just like them. You must deny them this. By finding a vocation that you can do well and can provide for your household glorifies God and does violence to the gates of Hell. More than anything else, that is what you must understand about vocation. Anyone can be a mercenary to feed their narcissistic desires, but the Christian man must pursue vocation as a sacrificial obligation to his household and to Christ's kingdom.

If you are a young, single man, and you make the self-conscious decision to establish a household, it is more attainable than if you come to that realization when you are older, but it is still very difficult. Not only do you need to want a household and have the ability to provide for it, but you need to find a young woman who also wants to have a household and to have one with you.

Modern women have been conditioned to see their slavery to globocorps as "liberation" because it comes with brunch and fur babies. So finding a young lady who has also discovered the extent to which the manufactured reality is depraved is an extremely difficult task. But, like you, they exist. If you pursue your mission, if you can secure a vocation that you like that can provide for a family, you must trust the Lord to find a good woman.

If you are older, and if you are already married, or married and with children, the task is considerably more difficult. Your spouse may be very comfortable with the modern arrangement. She may like having a dual income. She may like the conveniences of this world. Even if she is a Christian, she may hear things like "Wives, submit to your own husbands" and be catechized to make her submission conditional upon how much she thinks you love her like Christ loves the church. She may think raising up children in the nurture and admonition of the Lord means sending the kids to youth group once in a while. You must do what you can with what you have. If your wife is entrenched in feminism and love for Trashworld, you must be patient with her and seek to persuade her. You must build a household in exile. You must consciously understand, despite living in relative affluence, that you are in the position of an ancient slave who desires freedom, and even if you are in a position to attain it, you have a wife who clings to her slavery. What would a Christian do in that situation in the ancient world? He would devote all his energy to accomplishing this task no matter the cost. He would place his hope in the Lord fully in this endeavor. He would recognize that though there are many obstacles, the goal that he is pursuing is a thing that God has created him to accomplish. That is what you, too, must do. You must be patient with her.

You may have a wife who is fully on board with escaping her slavery to globohomo, but you are not in an economic position to do so. Every dollar she earns, your family budget needs. But here, at least you have a goal to pursue together, to build your income and cut your expenses so that you both can be devoted to the tasks of your household. It might be that she can at least work from home, and perhaps do so part-time. Do whatever you can to ensure that your children are raised in your own household as Christians, to grow and train little people to become conquerors.

If your children are grown, you can do what you can to help them escape their slavery. You can help them establish real households. If you live near them and are retired, you can help watch children or even assist with homeschooling. If you have the means to help them secure a home, you should do so. So many now retired people, who were among the first generations to be reared in this fictional consumerist world, will react, often angrily, that "Nobody helped us when we were your age." Yes, that is the problem. The household was already despised generations ago. You can either perpetuate the hatred of your own progeny, or you can reverse it to whatever extent you are able. Which is more important to you? That your grandchildren are not groomed to have their genitals removed or a second house in a warmer climate? You have worked extremely hard your entire life; the wealth you earned you really did earn. You were born in seven years of feasting, but now your children live in seven years of famine. The powers that rule you have exported millions of good jobs across the globe, and they have money printed your children into poverty. You can leave an inheritance to your children and your children's children—an inheritance that is actually having their own households—or you can enjoy a few more campsites in your RV, a few more rounds of golf, and a few more casts of your reel, all while your children and grandchildren are chewed up by a diabolic world. Will you go down to the grave thinking of that last putt you sunk or how your grandson will carry on your name with a house full of faithful Christians?

And if you are a Christian man of means, if God has given you wisdom, skill, and genius to build a successful business, what has He given that to you for? Has He blessed your labors so you can live in luxury while the world around you burns? Or has He made you a king so that you might be able to bless others to build faithful Christian households? Do you think Abraham's approach to his 318 fighting men was to calculate precisely what their utility to him was and pay them not one shekel more than that? Or was he a magnanimous prince who provided generously to his men so that they could build households of their own within his? The Christian man who God has blessed with success and the Christian man pursuing that success should have as their goal not merely the accumulation of wealth, but also the ability to provide Christian men with employment that can in turn provide for households. You must stop thinking of yourself as a mere individual but rather as a member of a hierarchy with duties and responsibilities to his people. The world that existed before Trashworld, the world Christendom existed within, had a word for men like this: nobles.

Any notion of hierarchy is abominable to the man who loves Trashworld. The ridiculous, fake historical lens the bugman views all through sees the natural hierarchy of the pre-modern world as a great monstrosity, that such men were abusive tyrants, but that was rarely the case. Instead these men lived under mutual obligations above them and below them. They were not mere individuals with a whole bunch of stuff. They had duties to kings above them and their people below them. It is not enough for you to accumulate enough wealth to escape the global liberal consumerist world, you must use all that God has given you to tear Trashworld down. And intentionally rebuilding a world in which men can provide for families is a sharpened chunk of iron striking the roots of world designed to drain men of their higher purpose.

The Household as the Means to Conquer Trashworld

The household is foundational to human existence, all the technological, economic, cultural, social, and political changes man can summon will never be able to change this immutable fact of reality. Doing what you can to live in conformity with how God has created the world, the way that He has created man and woman to live together, strikes at the heart of all the idols of the modern world. This is why your enemies have made it such a difficult thing to do. That is what you must remember when you are tempted to despair as you swim upstream while everyone around you tubes down the lazy river. Very few people will understand, much less celebrate, the strenuous and determined effort that you put forth as your sacrificial duty to your Lord and for your household.

When you live this way, you are making holy war against Christ's enemies. So be of good cheer. Be strong and courageous. Every email you send, every spreadsheet cell you fill, every load you drop off, every project you finish is one step closer to the gospel of Jesus Christ conquering the world.

CHAPTER 9
Brotherhood
Returning Man to the Human Way of Life

Two are better than one,
Because they have a good reward for their labor.
For if they fall, one will lift up his companion.
But woe to him who is alone when he falls,
For he has no one to help him up.
Again, if two lie down together, they will keep warm;
But how can one be warm alone?
Though one may be overpowered by another, two
* can withstand him.*
And a threefold cord is not quickly broken.

ECCLESIASTES 4:9–12

As we discussed in chapter 3, modern man is isolated, atomized, and alienated from all that which makes life meaningful. He is trapped in a sterile and synthetic world of concrete and plastic, and his social relations are similarly artificial. This programmed loneliness is as natural to human life as Astroturf. It is engineered to make Trashworld possible: the complex network of relationships that sustains human life are severed like a traumatic brain injury severs synapses. The individual is atomized in order to make political and social control of him effortless.

Just like so much else in the globohomo manufactured reality of which we are locked inside, all of it is built around intense, artificial forces that actively suppress the natural way of things. The entire globohomo project is a mammoth effort to get the Mississippi River to flow north. They have inverted the created order. We see this *everywhere*. This inversion of reality cannot be sustained without deliberate social isolation of as many individuals as possible, especially young people. Since they can make you feel alone and make you think *the whole rest of the planet* believes pigs can fly, if you even privately believe (much less publicly mention) that pigs are a landbound species, you will feel like you are going insane. Such things are not an accident of economic and technological forces moving inexorably and randomly. There are people with power who want things to be this way. Massive power has been exerted to get people to live in ways totally foreign to all of humanity for all of time. It is a colossal undertaking to get the Mississippi moving upstream. It takes the collective power of every institution in public life—media, entertainment, academia, finance, government, and even (especially!) churches—working in concert to force men who are created to exist in community to submit to and even prefer life in isolation. Under normative circumstances, forming friendships and existing within a community is the natural state of man. People want to get married. People want to start families. People want to have children. People want to have friends and be part of groups. An unbelievable amount of energy and effort is expended to repress these desires that God has created men to have, but no matter how hard they rage against the created order, it remains.

They can chop off a man's penis and testicles, leaving a lasting and festering wound that they pretend is a vagina. They can give him silicone breast implants. They can give him female hormones. But no matter what they do, no matter how much they mangle and mar what he is, no matter how much they make him look like one of Sid's toys from *Toy Story*, no matter how grotesque they make him, every cell in his body remains uniquely male. No matter what they do to his outward appearance, he is a man. The same is true for society as a whole. No matter how much they disfigure it, no matter what monstrous surgeon's scalpel wounds it bears, no matter how much they contort it into something hideous, it retains the nature of what God has made it.

The job of the reformer is to grab hold of our figuratively trans-ed society's XY chromosomes and not let go. No matter how much people have been memed and psyopsed into believing they are introverts and conditioned to practice antisocial behaviors, people want to love and be loved. Men and women were designed to *not* be alone. No one *wants* to feel like nobody cares about them. Knowing this is a weapon against globohomo; a weapon that you personally can wield powerfully against this hideous, decrepit world.

De-Atomizing by Repairing Your Relationships with Family

To begin with, in your own life, you have family. You have people you are related to. They might still be trapped in this fake and gay trans-ed world. They might still believe everything the TV says to them. They might have made movie or sports fandom (or political fandom) and consuming product as a replacement for anything meaningful in their lives. Your duty is to be patient with them. Your duty is not to argue with them or be repulsed by their deep loyalty to this fictional reality. Their attachment to it exists in part because they have no flesh and blood people to transfer that loyalty to. They are that way because they (at least perceive) they don't have anyone who truly loves them.

Your duty is to love your family. To repair relationships that have been undone by sin and bitterness and envy and betrayal, sometimes for decades. You must forgive your father for his failures and his foibles and his sins against you. Whatever he has done, you must not hold it against him. You must show him that you respect him and hold him in high regard, even if that respect has not been earned. You must hold no bitterness toward your mother, no matter what she has said or done to you. You must forgive her and show her you love her, even if she does not deserve it. You must forgive your siblings for however they have sinned against you and do what you can to give them time and attention you have withheld from them.

You must repent of your envy for the success they have had that you have not attained, and you must repent of delighting in their envy of success you have they have not attained. All of this is sacrifice. You will be giving of yourself in ways that you should not expect to be reciprocated, at least immediately. You must do hard, often painful work to repair damaged familial relationships in your own life, and in doing so you are personally sabotaging a system designed to make human life as miserable as possible.

But going out of your way to sacrificially repair familial relationships does not just have an effect on those particular family members, but it will strengthen family bonds between you and people who have not even been born yet. Reforging the strong bonds of love between you and previous generations will bear fruit in future generations as well. You should want your children to be born into strong extended families, to know and love and be loved by their great-grandparents, grandparents, aunts, uncles, and a legion of cousins. This was way of life for nearly everyone ever born until the twentieth century, but now it is seemingly only the experience of micro-societies frozen in time like the Amish. To be born into a people who love you and whom you love is a massive blessing that is withheld from the overwhelming majority of our society. To begin now to do all that you personally can to repair the damage the last fifty years have done to your family is work that will pay dividends for generations that will never even know your name.

This is why the idea of having children has been intentionally socially engineered out of people. The natural impulse to produce offspring has been carefully and deliberately severed from sexual desire, all the cultural and social mores governing sex that funneled the young toward family formation have been demolished. This is why a life of perpetual adolescence is glorified. All of our young people have been psyopsed into adopting the fruitless, nihilistic, and consumeristic lifestyle of the homosexual, whether or not their hearts have been groomed into those particular sexual perversions. The intentionally childless, consumerist, permanent adolescent is gay, whether he sexually desires his same sex or not. It is important for us to be aware that this has been programmed into the hearts of the young, so that we can teach our children to hate it. It is simply not enough to keep your kids from watching movies or having access to the internet when they are in your home. No matter what you do, the magical dark liturgy that runs twenty-four seven will still be out there, and the likelihood that your children will have FOMO (fear of missing out) will be high. But teaching your children to hate it is far more important than keeping it hidden away from them. They should learn specifically why they ought to despise everything from Trashworld. In your house they should mature to recognize that the glories of this disgusting world of ugliness are nothing but hideous monstrosities.

Fighting Back by Building True Brotherhood

You and your family cannot exist in isolation. In combating this world of filth, it is not enough to swim against the antinatalist social engineering by simply having a lot of children. Those who slip past the childfree-and-loving-it programming are dealt with by having the hearts and souls of those children stolen. You must teach your children to love the things you love and hate the things you hate. You must overcome your aversion to *hate*. If you cannot bring yourself to hate a malignant world built upon child sacrifice and crowned with child genital mutilation, you are not going to make it, nor will your children. Hatred of such things is something that you must pass down to your children, and you must raise them among others who understand the same. The network of friends and family you interact with regularly is the soil your children are growing in. If they are alone and isolated, if the only friends they have are entranced with Trashworld, no matter how much effort you expend homeschooling and keeping evil things from their eyes, they will be vulnerable. More than anything, you and your wife and your children need friends who love what you love and hate what you hate.

This world that has stripped humanity of the things that make us human so that you think the place where you live is merely a function of bare economic utility. You live wherever you can make money. But for all of human history the *place* you live was never merely a function of economic determinism. Yes, economics is not irrelevant to discussion of place; sometimes there was a famine in the land and you have to go somewhere else. But apart from being utterly unable to survive in a place, very little dislodged people from where they were from. When I teach the Bible, I must often repaint premodern social life for people. When we get to the passage where Jesus is rejected by His hometown, I have to stop and explain to people that until just a few generations ago, most families lived in the same village for hundreds of years. Everyone there knew your cousins, grandfather, great-uncles, and so on, and you knew theirs. The people in Jesus's hometown know Him intimately, which makes them unable to *truly* know Him. Such a thing is nearly impossible for modern suburbanite people to fathom. Having a place where you are from and where you belong, having a people you belong to are incredibly potent forces grounding you in reality. Being cut off from place, people, and inherited tradition and being made totally rootless—something like an economic migrant with a mortgage—is a cause of untold destruction. In order to conquer this disgusting world, we must restore love of people and place, we must physically move closer to those who share the same loves and hates we do. Your children need a people to belong to, they need a tribe, they need bonds of friendship even stronger than blood.

This is why it is of the utmost importance that you learn how to make friends. Yes, it seems absurd to even say such a thing, but in the current age it must be said. If this horrid world has been designed to make social isolation the default position for young people that following the path of least resistance naturally results in, you need to go out of your way to counteract this. You need to reject the antisocial impulses that you have been conditioned by. You need to spend your time meeting people with similar interests, getting to know people at your gym, going to Bible studies, going to the gun range, joining clubs. If in the land of the blind the one-eyed man is king, in an atomized, isolated, antisocial generation, the man who takes an active interest in engaging everyone he meets will rule. If voting is even somewhat of a cultural barometer, there are tens of millions of people in the United States who have shown at least some resistance to Trashworld. Your enemy wants you and them to feel like they are completely on an island and everything they hold dear is a battle *contra mundum*. If you have ever fought a battle where it was you against everyone else, you know how discouraging and exhausting that is. In such circumstances, there is nothing more powerful that knowing somebody, *anybody* is on your side. There are few greater expressions of love than standing side by side with a friend, backs against the wall, *contra mundum*— against the world.

The great vulnerability of Trashworld is how much social isolation is required to get people to love the total inversion of what is true, good, and beautiful. A group of ten to twelve men, who would die for one another is a thing that is more powerful than an entire division of conscripts. With such a group churches can be planted that can conquer entire cities. As soon as you bring people into contact with a church filled with men who have good relationships with their fathers and mothers and sisters and brothers, men who have wives and sons and daughters who love them and they shower with love, and men who they can see have other men who love them so much they would die for them, no matter how much their heart and mind has been scrambled by a lifetime of intense social conditioning, it is difficult to escape the gravitational pull of actual love. People desperately want to belong and to love and feel love. If you build a place where it is impossible to deny that love exists, you have built a nuclear-powered woodchipper for the grotesque shrines of this age.

CHAPTER 10
Made for War
Rekindling Masculine Vitality

Be watchful, stand firm in the faith, act like men, be strong.

1 CORINTHIANS 16:13 (ESV)

"What is more sublime than facing certain death at the head of a hundred men."

ERNST JUNGER, *THE STORM OF STEEL*

As we have repeatedly seen above, Trashworld is designed to invert the created order. God created men to be strong and able to exert force. God created men for war. Trashworld has actively made men weak, fat, and impotent. This is not something that only effects a man's physical body. God created man's body, mind, and spirit as an integrated whole. If you are physically unable to physically impose your will upon the world, this will also be manifested mentally and physically as well. God created you to have the body, mind, and spirit of a warrior.

The fetid modern world of filth has horribly disfigured the very image of man. We must break free from the way of life Trashworld has imposed upon men to recover the very nature of what God made us to be. This chapter is devoted to provide means where we can begin this recovery. Throughout I will speak in general terms that can be applied to most particular situations, but your mileage may vary. What I can do, however, is speak from my own experience. I, too, was once a consumer of the Standard American Diet. I once topped the scales at more than three bills. But as I began to realize Trashworld for what it is, I recognized being fat, weak, and sickly was not how God had created me to live. I had to fight against every impulse to pursue the path of least resistance to Trashworld and pursue another course. I began to transform my diet and entire manner of life. I began to train regularly and consistently with a barbell. I began to hate every part of this world that is designed to create the expectation that strong, fit, and beautiful men are the very rare exception and not the baseline. This is also what you must do, and I hope to show a pathway toward this in what follows.

How Did God Create Man in the First Place?

To begin with, we have to start with how God created man. Men have been castrated by Trashworld's inversion of reality socially, economically, politically, culturally, biologically, hormonally, and in some cases literally. God created our father, the first man, Adam, to guard and keep God's garden sanctuary. When many Christian leaders teach on the book of Genesis, they often breeze right past this, subtly assuming it means that the very purpose of masculinity is to be a horticulturalist.

But that is not what those words mean. The word often translated in English as "keep" in Genesis 2:15 is the Hebrew word *somrah*. The exact same word is used in the next chapter to describe the cherubim who "guarded" the way to the Tree of Life. After Adam fails to guard the garden from the serpent and is banished, the cherubim replace him in this function. His purpose is not to keep the Garden like your grandma in her straw sun hat holding pruning shears. His job is that of a warrior-priest, to kill anything that transgresses the sanctuary. Adam was created for holy war. He was created to employ violence to protect the sanctuary. He was created to be a warrior priest. It is a task that he failed at and only that great warrior king, the Second Adam, Jesus Christ, succeeded in. Nevertheless, this is what he and you, his sons, were created to be. God designed your body, your arms, your legs, your torso, your fingers, your mind, your soul, and your spirit for war.

But Trashworld has been designed to take all of this away from you. Not even to speak of the social and economic conditions that have reduced men to lonely, miserable cuckolds and geldings, the very biology of man has been marred and made unrecognizable. You were not created to be flabby, saggy, and weak. You were not created to be bloated and unable to move without robotic support, like Baron Harkonnen in *Dune*. The outward appearance of the men deformed by this hideous world reveals what has happened to men internally—men have become fragile, weak, passive, extremely agreeable and conflict averse, and cowardly. This is the default spiritual state of the modern bugman. He is usually obese, and if not that, he is nevertheless devoid of any developed musculature and he has the emotional maturity of a prepubescent child. This is literally a description of eunuchs from the ancient world. Eunuchs, especially if they were gelded before puberty, never had requisite testosterone to produce muscle mass. This along with the kind of access to calories found in a palace made them something unique in the premodern world—extremely obese. They were men who are not quite men; men who are not a physical threat to other men, but are instead destructive in their capacity for conniving and scheming. If you simply live the way you are expected to live in our inversion of reality, this is what you will become. All of our ancestors were just born and lived and went about their lives and they grew into men who looked like and truly were men. Today, it takes tremendous effort and strength of will simply to bear the same physical appearance all men for all time took for granted. But it is an effort that you absolutely must make.

You Need to Be Getting Smaller

The odds are extremely high you need to lose body fat. There is no way around this. More than anything else obesity is almost certainly the primary cause of your low testosterone, your physical weakness, and your feeble emotional state. How this is accomplished is different for everyone. There is no shortage of hacks and fad diets for sale, looking to take advantage of your desire to not be fat but also to exert the least amount of effort, feel the absolute minimum pain, and require absolutely no discipline. You should avoid the temptation to get things the easy way; an entire lifetime of the easy way is the reason your pants no longer fit. The plan that works to stop being fat is the one you will actually consistently do. But you must know you will feel hunger, you will want to give up, but for the sake of yourself, your family, your children, your church, and your people you must do everything you can to rid yourself of the bodyfat that is the visible mark of your entrapment in bugworld.

The causes of obesity are difficult to pin down, but many have pointed to the widespread consumption of industrial seed oils.[1] Industrialization of our food supply is a blessing to the extent that it efficiently delivers calories to an ever-increasing population, but these processes that produce food at such a massive scale have introduced

---

1. The best resource on the topic of industrial seed oils as cause of obesity, and the need to return to traditional diets can be found in Catherine Shanahan, *Deep Nutrition: Why Your Genes Need Traditional Food* (New York: Flatiron Books, 2018).

kinds of foods and changes to nutrition that have never been seen before in human history. Whether good or bad, we have only seen food production like this for only one or two full generations, and it is no coincidence that we have had an exponential rise in obesity. When the scale is so dramatically increased and an industry is so heavily financialized that a fraction of a percent to profit margins means tens of millions of dollars per year, it is reasonable to wonder if our food has been adulterated. Could replacing animal fat in our diet with a thing that a hundred years ago was only fit to be used as paint thinner—seed oils—be a significant cause of what is making us both flabby and ill, sapping us of all masculine energy? What if our entire food supply is designed not to provide the necessary nutrition to sustain life, but primarily to increase the consumption of food and thereby increase profits?

The fact remains that we live in an age of universal deceit. They have told you that the foods that made your ancestors healthy and strong—eggs, red meat, butter—are all killing you. These are lies. They want you to live in a gnostic fantasy world where your sustenance is totally divorced from the created order: you will eat industrial sludge derived from soybeans and insects and you will love it—or else. They do not want you to consume foods that have come from the animals God gave us to both rule over and to thankfully feast on. Everyone has seen man-on-the-street videos of low-IQ city dwellers who sincerely believe milk and meat simply comes from the grocery store. Those who rule over us want *everyone* to be that disconnected from reality. Even the meme-ideology of veganism is a symptom of this. The fact is that most vegans, while rightly concerned about the poor treatment of animals in industrial food complex, are totally naive about just how much animal death is required to keep their kale, soybeans, grains, and fruit from being consumed by insects and pests before it is available to them. Who can forget the urban garden planted in the early days of the Capitol Hill Autonomous Zone during the BLM riots of 2020, with lettuce hilariously sown in half an inch of topsoil? The modern world has been constructed to make you as clueless as possible about what food is and where it comes from. They want you as disconnected from reality as possible. They want you to have absolutely no idea about what sustains human life.

The closer you are to the immutable realities of the created order, the harder the fake transhumanist reality is for them to foist upon you. But if you are a bugman, living in a pod, totally comfortable with a lifetime of consuming food with at least fifty unpronounceable, sciency-sounding ingredients that came out of an assembly line, getting you to submit to utopian horrors is not that hard.

But eating food someone had to kill, eating food a human being took out of the ground, eating food that all of humanity throughout all of time would recognize as food places you back within the world God made. To do so regularly is an assault on the idols of this decrepit, revolting age. To eat the kind of food your great-great grandmother would make you if you went back in time and showed up for dinner is to put an ax to the root of so much that is horrible. Simply consciously changing the way you eat is a radical assault against those who rule over you, and it is no coincidence that there is such an intense push to introduce even more grotesque abominations like imitation meat. They want you to be simultaneously obese and malnourished. They want you to have low testosterone. The future they want for you is to be an immobile slug plugged into a virtual reality of endless entertainment and porn attached to a feeding tube filling you with a smoothie of canola oil and cockroaches. This is the present reality for many already, just with extra steps. You must resolve to break out of this prison.

The Barbell as the Key Out of Trashworld
Changing your diet is one means to break free of the transhumanist slave state, but it is not the only thing you should do. Once you have overcome an objectively unhealthy diet, you will begin to feel the changes in your body. You will begin to regain a sense of true autonomy. A truly free man is a man capable of protecting his family and his home with physical violence; a free man is a dangerous man. In ancient Israel, unless God raised up men who could use physical violence to repel invaders, the people were in bondage even in their own land. In

Judges 6, Israel lived in artificial famine because of Midianite occupation until God raised up Gideon to kill them and drive them out. Among the ancient Greeks, the main social distinction between free men and slaves was that slaves were not allowed to physically train. It is suicidal for a slave state to allow slaves to become dangerous and capable of revolt. Take a look around you at the world you see and you will see nothing but millions of men who could not threaten a fly, physically weak men, men who have been fattened and emasculated by social engineers who want millions of expendable slaves they consider human filth. They do not want you capable of running a mile without huffing and puffing halfway through. They do not want you able to pick up twice your bodyweight or more. They do not want you to be dangerous.

It is not an accident that the two things they closed down most zealously during the lockdowns of 2020 were churches and gyms. They do not want you to be spiritually healthy any more than they want you to be physically healthy. A spiritually healthy and physically fit people are an impediment to the abominations they desire. When you have, through much toil and struggle, adapted your body to the conditions of this world that God has made, you are, whether you are consciously aware of it or not, grounded in reality. The ability to physically impose your will upon the world, even in small ways, even picking up more and more weight off the ground radically changes your perception of reality. You are no longer a helpless waif tossed to and fro by forces far beyond your control. You realize you have agency. You have the ability to conquer even the small spaces within your grasp. Making yourself as physically strong as you possibly can is not about vanity, it is about restoring yourself to manhood, becoming an Adam that can make war in guarding and protecting the garden. You must shape yourself into a weapon, instill in yourself the discipline to resemble a man of war. God designed you to be strong and courageous (1 Cor. 16:13). The glory of young men is their strength (Prov. 20:29). Men with the spirit of holy war within them will be what brings down the idols of this fetid, corpulent, repulsive world.

CHAPTER 11
A New Eve
Resurrecting the Unique Glory of the Woman

> "... but woman is the glory of man. For man is not from woman, but woman from man. Nor was man created for the woman, but woman for the man.
>
> 1 CORINTHIANS 11:7B-9

Feminism is at the heart of Trashworld's rebellion against the Triune God and the reduction of all that is good, true, and beautiful into a heap of excrement and filth. The assault on God's created order, that is in furious rebellion against everything that He has established, finds its apex in the destruction of the distinction between man and woman. If the immutable boundary that is so fundamental to the image of God—male and female He created them—can be transgressed, *anything* and *everything* can and will be done. By ripping the deep-seated, natural, creational desire to marry and have children from women, by leveling all distinctions between man and woman, and by reducing women to mere human beings, do the masters of this decrepit age make normal, peaceful, well-ordered human life impossible. If you destroy the femininity of woman, if you mangle what it means to be a wife, if you contort and disfigure motherhood, you have transformed the womb and the household into a factory for the production of bugmen.

Recovering the Lost Knowledge of a Forgotten Civilization

In our destruction of the idolatries, we must understand that while it is incredibly difficult to tear idols down, it is even more difficult to rebuild the things that are good, true, and beautiful. We are living in the ruins of a collapsed civilization, and the knowledge of "how do you have a family?" has been totally lost. After Rome collapsed, the knowledge and ability to do certain types of metallurgy, to manufacture certain combinations of metals, was completely lost. All the men who knew how to make pewter or steel simply just died off without passing that knowledge on to anyone.

The entire concept of how to have a household, which had been transmitted for countless generations as if by osmosis, has simply disappeared. No one went to school to study household formation. You just observed how it had been done and replicated that knowledge. No young woman had to read a dozen books on how to be a wife or mother or how to raise a child or even what it meant to be a woman. This knowledge was passed down to you, often without a word about it being said.

During the lockdowns, every young woman I know, including my wife, started making sourdough bread. Toilet paper had disappeared, and no one knew if the bread on the shelf would be next. The position we are in today is as if society had collapsed, and the trucks had stopped coming with food, and not one single person knew how to produce food anymore. All the lessons of generations of farmers and cooks had been completely lost. We would have to re-learn the lessons of trial and error that untold generations had already figured out for us. But not all *is* lost. To continue the metaphor, like monks discovering a lost codex with a recipe for making sourdough and explaining the process to the baker, God's Word has at least a basic framework for recovering lost womanhood and the rebuilding the household.

In 1 Timothy 4, the Apostle Paul gave instructions to his disciple Timothy, who led the church in Ephesus. One of the questions that required apostolic authority to solve was what to do with younger widows. Presupposed in his answer is the existence of the household and the distinct roles of man and woman, husband and wife. Paul's concern was that if young widows were enrolled into the care and service of the church (because they had no husband to provide for them), they would become idle busybodies and even forsake the faith. His instruction to Timothy was to have them remarry instead—to bear children, manage their households, and live above reproach. The entire answer presupposed the normality of the household and the woman's role within it.

Elsewhere, Paul commands his disciple in Crete, Titus, in Titus 2:4–5, to instruct the older women in the church to encourage the young women to show affection to their husbands and children, to be discreet and chaste, to manage their households, to pursue excellence, and to obey their husbands. As in 1 Timothy, Paul isn't commanding that these things be brought into existence where there had been nothing; he is presupposing marriage, the household, and the distinct roles for husband and wife within that household. He is instructing Christian women how to live in a way that is not at odds with the order God created in the world. The passages (along with Ephesians 5–6) presuppose a thing that in our monstrously adulterous age has been ripped apart.

In order to conform such passages to Trashworld, the bugman has to say Paul was just wrong, *or* he must assert that any moral instruction in the Bible is dependent upon cultural context and therefore we can pick and choose what is valid *or* he must contort and manipulate it so badly through super-academic, crafty exegesis that only the most respectable scholars can even begin to sift through, showing that Paul is not really giving any instruction at all that anyone without decades of training in the minutiae of Greek grammar can ever hope to discern. But the plain teaching of the Bible is very clear: widowed young women should marry, have children, manage a household, and live a godly, Christian life. And if that is his instruction to young *widows*, how easy it to apply to young women *in general*! It was simply assumed by the apostle that this is what young women ordinarily did; they got married, had children, and managed households. For Paul, having the church support the young widows was not an option; neither did the apostle say to the young widows, bereft of husbands to support them, "Go sell yourself into slavery. That way, you'll have something to eat." This was an option in first-century Ephesus, just as selling years of future labor to be an accountant or registered nurse is today, if you think about it. For Paul, forming a household was the solution of the question of what to do with all of these unmarried single (widowed) women of childbearing age in the church.

The church today faces a similar problem. Our young people are not getting married, and as easy as it is to blame young single guys for not manning up and putting away their video games, you have to reckon with the social situation of the world our young people have been reared in. *Everyone* believes you should not get married until you are established in your career, and, increasingly, getting established in your career takes longer and longer for young men today as the bottom rungs on the economic and social mobility ladder are sawn off. And young women from even the most conservative churches are not immune from the more general milieu, where young girls are able to enjoy the consumeristic benefits of wage slavery, brunches, mimosas, Instagrammable vacations, etc., all without ever having to *submit* to a dirty, stinky man. And this is often the best-case scenario, where the young ladies are committed to a Christian sexual ethic of chastity. For the non-Christian counterparts to our Christian young woman in this Gomorrah, the situation is drastically more bleak: unlimited sexual liaisons with strangers are only a swipe away, and it is not uncommon for her to have had dozens or even hundreds of men inside her.[1] This is the way of life the masters of this pit of filth have constructed for young women.

That is the point that must be brought home in the clearest terms possible: our daughters are given the option of being wives and mothers and builders of households that will bring forth a glorious heritage for generations to come *or* being receptacles for the seed of a hundred different men. What were they created to be? Which option gives them dignity, purpose, and fulfillment? To birth, feed, nurture, and raise up new people and bring greater and greater glory to her household or

1. "National Survey of Family Growth," Centers for Disease Control, https://www.cdc.gov/nchs/nsfg/key_statistics/n-keystat.htm. In 2019, over 50 percent of women aged 25–49 have had five or more sexual partners, over 25 percent have had more than ten, and 13 percent have had fifteen or more.

to be a meat-puppet sex toy for countless random men who will give her rapidly diminishing attention after her twenty-eighth birthday? This is what must be presented to our young women and our daughters: that the options before you are either household or harlotry.

Are there outliers and exceptions to the get married and have kids principle? *Of course there are.* But if you focus on the what-ifs, you are missing the point. Trashworld is designed to actively funnel our daughters into its degrading lifestyle. The gravitational pull of Tinder and OnlyFans, shaking her body parts for TikTok, and living-for-brunch is unbelievably intense. You must understand: fear of missing out is a sword of Damocles perpetually hanging over your daughter's head. You must teach her to hate the thing Trashworld wants her to love, but that is not enough.

The Millstone to Crush the Head of Trashworld: Loving Motherhood

You must give her something to love and desire that kills any desire to miss out on Trashworld. She must see what all her great-great-grandmothers saw: that the joy of bringing new men and women into the world is a unique privilege that God has given specifically to her that she should cherish, that she has been given something precious that not everyone can do, that she will one day bring forth little kings and queens who will one day rule. Why would she want to trade that for filling her day with spreadsheets between pointless, empty sex with guys who won't even text her back?

If we are to rebuild Christian civilization, if we are to ever recover the things that have been lost, we need our young women to be willing to exchange the fleeting pleasures of Trashworld for the riches of rebuilding a new world. It will require a willing embrace of suffering, not just the pain of childbearing, but the pain and difficulty and the struggle and toil of childrearing, and a willingness to bear the relative poverty designed to discourage family formation. Every woman in your lineage born before your great-grandmother brought children into the world under tremendous pain, and at significant risk to her life. Every time she got pregnant, she knew there were substantial odds that bearing this child would claim her life. If she survived each pregnancy, her baby had a 25 percent chance of not living to say his first word and a 50 percent chance of not living to adulthood. Life in the premodern world was dangerous. Death was always in the foreground and not hidden away as it is today. Only when the perceived threat of a deadly pandemic did our society briefly remember death stalks us all, and look at the chaos this resulted in. But now, despite its never being easier and safer to deliver a child and raise him to adulthood, motherhood has never been more despised. Your female ancestors risked their lives to bear children they knew they would likely weep and mourn over, and the women of Trashworld fear a child might cut into brunch time.

Our duty in this idolatrous age is to raise courageous women like those we are descended from. Women who understand they have been uniquely *blessed* with a call to a special sort of warfare. The battle she fights is through much pain, toil, and grief, and it is all to her glory, which is to bring future generations into the world. Trashworld seeks to entice your daughters to desire *anything* but *that*.

To teach your daughters to hate those enticements, you must make your own household a place of deep joy. It must be a refuge from the disgusting world of filth. A place your daughters would give their lives to replicate. If your household is a place of strife, a place they cannot wait to flee from, no matter how much time, effort, and wealth you expend to raise your child in the nurture and admonition of the Lord, you are doing the job of Trashworld and you may as well sign your daughter up for OnlyFans yourself. Every single thing you do in raising your daughters, whether you do it well or poorly, is a tiny step closer to her answering the ultimate question of what she will do with her life: household or harlotry? You must be present and give her the attention you don't even realize she craves. Every second you devote your focus to your daughter is an investment that will bear a ten-thousandfold return. Even when your daughter is in diapers, every moment you consciously devote to her is more money in the bank directing her toward a life that is in conformity with the order of the world that God created, and away from the promiscuous, degenerate anti-life of Trashworld.

You do not realize the power that the decisions you make in mundane daily life has in affecting the future of the world. Your sphere of influence, especially if you are a husband and a father, has the power to lay waste to the repulsive idolatries of this world of gangrenous rot. You have each day the privilege and duty to shape and form new Eves who are conformed to the image of the Second Adam, Jesus Christ. You are producing the people who will literally birth Christian civilization as the empire of filth comes crashing down around you. And all it takes is setting down your phone and looking your girls in the eyes.

CHAPTER 12
The Paideia of Christendom
Shaping a People Who Will Conquer

And you, fathers, do not provoke your children to wrath, but bring them up in the paideia and admonition of the Lord.
EPHESIANS 6:4.

By now you are aware you have been robbed. You must recover that which was stolen from you and your posterity.

There is no other way of saying it. The history, tradition, literature, and art that shaped the men and women who built cathedrals, discovered continents, founded nations, and produced exponentially greater wealth than any human civilization had ever seen, has been totally withheld from you and your children. There may have been dribs and drabs of it you were allowed to see. You maybe got to see the *Wishbone* version of *The Odyssey* in fourth grade English class. You might have read an abridged version of *Romeo and Juliet*. You may have even learned the Old Testament by watching *VeggieTales*. But you do not *know* the things that made the people who built the city whose ruins you live in.

What you *do* know is the mythology of *Star Wars*, *Harry Potter*, the Marvel Cinematic Universe, and whatever the History Channel might have told you about World War II. You have been allowed access to the myths that form the moral imagination of the bugman, but to know the history of the people you came from, to what they understood to be true, good, and beautiful, to share in what they loved, what they hated, what they honored, what they held in derision, what gave their hearts cheer and filled them with laughter—*that* has been withheld from you. You may not have this secret knowledge. You may not know what things made your great-great-great-great grandfather who and what he was. You are only allowed to know how disabled black trans lesbian Jedi Knights saved Handmaids from being forced to have babies begotten by Voldemort and Thanos.

While the cultural inheritance of Christendom has been totally redacted from the popular consciousness like Amenhotep IV's name being chiseled off the pyramids, they have not been able to eradicate all evidence of it. This is one reason why Ivy League and other universities still have classics departments (and divinity schools for that matter). Their job is to convince you that Plato and Aristotle were pink-haired genderqueer POCs. Their function is to teach you that the only applicable moral teaching of the Bible is that all seven billion people on planet earth have a human right to live in the United States, to vote in American elections, and to demand everyone use their preferred pronouns. They have to do this kind of violence to the classical and Christian tradition because they will never be able to fully eradicate the literature of antiquity and historical Christianity. They have to obscure and disfigure it instead.

Recovering the Lost Tools of Conquest

This might seem extremely depressing to consider. It should instead be something that gives you great confidence. Even if only the stump remains of our heritage, they will never be able to kill off the shoots springing up. Even if they douse the great fire of our Christian civilization, they will never be able to put out the embers. And this should be a great encouragement to you. If you are reading this, you have it within your power to recover something ancient, something lost, and most of all, something very powerful. You personally have the ability to preserve the great heritage being lost. By reading Thucydides, Homer, Virgil, Plutarch, Saint Augustine, and others and by having your children learn their heritage, you are functioning in the very same way as monks who painstakingly preserved the cultural inheritance of the Western world. You will be guarding and keeping the great garden from which men like Charles Martel, Charlemagne, and Alfred arose—men that made the work of missionaries like Saint Boniface possible.

You should be reading and listening to the great works of Western tradition. You can recover that which was stolen from you. While there are downsides to the internet, there has never been greater access to the wealth of historical knowledge and literature of Christendom. You have the ability to walk into the Library of Alexandria at your fingertips, yet you would rather binge at the swine trough of Hulu. Yes, learning these things as an adult will take time and effort. You will have to go well out of your way to do this. You will likely not be able to go back to college much less grammar school, but there has never been more access to ancient knowledge at your fingertips. You must look at this as though you are an irredentist nobleman, raising an army to take back the homeland that is rightfully his. Yes, it should have been simply given to you, but you will have to fight for it instead. But you must understand, knowing the history of your people and knowing all that they loved and hated and what moved them to great passion is a powerful weapon.

This is why the architects of this Trashworld have purposely withheld it from you and your children. They don't want you to share the same things that built the first Christendom. They want you rootless. They want to shape your moral imagination by increasingly perverted and inane entertainment. Denying this from them, and instead drinking deeply from the fount of Christendom will hasten their defeat. You should be reading classical literature. You should be reading the all the volumes of Will and Ariel Durant, all the works of John Julius Norwich, and, more recently, men such as Roger Scruton and Tom Holland. Your children should be learning Latin and Greek. And, above all else, you should know the Bible. Even if you do this poorly (by the standards of what an educated man was prior to the mid-twentieth century) you and your children will be vastly better educated than nearly everyone alive, including (and especially) our truly unimpressive intellectual elite.

Christian *Paideia* as a Parallel Society

It is in the *paideia* of Christendom that the men who will refound our civilization will be formed. And it is the duty of every Christian to forge his children in this crucible. That word, *paideia*, is often translated in Paul's Epistle to the Ephesians as "training," "nurture," or "discipline." As Douglas Wilson aptly points out, based upon the word's usage in the totality of extant ancient Greek literature, entire volumes could be written outlining its meaning, much like *democracy* today.[1] *Paideia* is the complete and total immersion and incorporation

---

1. Wilson, Douglas, *The Case for Classical Christian Education* (Moscow, ID: Canon Press, 2022), 117ff.

of a person into a particular way of life. But even in the ancient and pre-modern world, this simply did not happen by osmosis—it took training, discipline, and work. A child in the paideia of Christendom was actively formed and shaped by it.

Therefore, if you wish to break free of Trashworld, it is imperative that your children receive the education of Christendom. You must do all that you can to liberate them from the government internment day camps, where they are at their greatest danger of physical and sexual assault, and where their souls are in extreme danger of total destruction. There is no gentle way to put this: the public school is the incubator of the bugman. It is the *paideia* of globohomo. If you were to tell someone this even three years ago, they would have taken you for a schizophrenic lunatic, but since the Wuhan flu, when parents began to see the kind of content their children were being exposed to and the kind of people doing the exposing, a significant number of people have become willing to listen who otherwise would not. Combine this with intentional efforts to groom children into homosexuality and transgenderism, often without parental knowledge. As of 2022, nearly 20 percent of Gen Z adults claim to be gay, lesbian, bisexual, or transgender.[2] We are now to the point that children are having puberty disrupted or even their genitals removed without their parents knowledge or consent. This is something that is

2. Jeffrey M. Jones, "U.S. LGBT Identification Steady at 7.2%," Gallup, https://news.gallup.com/poll/470708/lgbt-identification-steady.aspx.

rightly striking fear into the hearts of many who otherwise implicitly trusted "our schools." Everyone knows public school teachers that they love and respect, and this is a major reason why, despite objective and precipitous decline in educational results, until now "our schools" remained one of the most trusted institutions in the country. But the prospect of your son coming home from school without his penis nullifies the trust you have in your friend the history teacher and football coach that you know is a good guy.

For the reformer, for the man who would tear down the idols of this age, that we have reached this inflection point is a good thing. The frogs that still have nerve endings left are beginning to feel their skin get scalded. If they jump out of the pot only to do the *paideia* of Trashworld at home (but without the grooming), they are simply jumping from a boiling pot to a simmering one. You must give them the alternative. You must advocate for what was lost. You must do all that you can to promote the *paideia* of Christendom. You can devote yourself to building homeschool co-ops. You can and must build Christian schools. Our children will be like the monks of the Middle Ages who spent their lives painstakingly making copies of all the knowledge of the Classical World as the world around them burned down. It will take a lifetime of work, but these parallel institutions can *and must* be built. When you have done this, you will have raised an army of Bonifaces to chop down the idolatries of this disgusting, adulterous age.

Conclusion

> *Then out spoke brave Horatius, the Captain of the Gate:*
> *"To every man upon this earth, death cometh soon or late;*
> *And how can man die better than facing fearful odds,*
> *For the ashes of his fathers, and the temples of his Gods . . . ?"*
>
> "HORATIUS" THOMAS BABBINGTON MACAULAY

The Way Forward

This is the Boniface Option: that you see the antihuman dystopia you live in for what it is, that you recognize you will never be able to run from it, and that you confront it, first within yourself and then everywhere else. You cannot flee to a Benedict Option community and think you and your family will be safe there. Trashworld is everywhere. You may need to withdraw to a better strategic location, but only as a warrior understands retreat for the purpose of later offensive action.

God has called you to spend the one life that He has given you to work to rebuild Christian civilization within your sphere of influence; to build strong brotherhoods with other men committed to doing the same; to shape your body, mind, and soul into being the kind of men capable of overthrowing empires; and to set your spirit on fire with the very same flame that once engulfed most of the planet in the glories of Christendom.

The world we now live in has now become hostile not just to the Christian faith, but even to created order itself. Trashworld is a world of tremendous sickness. There have been a few helpful ways to describe these conditions. Aaron Renn has offered a threefold schema that he calls Positive World, Neutral World, and Negative World.[1] In short, Positive World is where the Christian religion is viewed as a social positive, i.e., if you are publicly known as a Christian, this will be beneficial to your social status and career. Whereas in Neutral World, your public faith is neither beneficial nor detrimental, and in Negative World it is entirely detrimental to your social status and economic prospects. Renn's framing is

1. Aaron Renn, "The Three Worlds of Evangelicalism" First Things, (February 2022). https://www.firstthings.com/article/2022/02/the-three-worlds-of-evangelicalism.

an accurate description of the situation, and he freely admits the only strategy put forward for Christians now living in Negative World is the Dreher's aforementioned *Benedict Option*, which he (rightly) describes as pessimistic,[2] and which I believe is totally unworkable, at least as Dreher has presented it. But it is no longer the only strategy: it is time for the Boniface Option.

Another framing of the thing that I have sardonically described throughout as Trashworld, bugworld, globohomo, and this disgusting world of filth, is Philip Reiff's confusingly named first world/second world/third world system from his *Sacred Order/Social Order* (frequently referenced by Carl Trueman in *The Rise and Triumph of the Modern Self*).[3] Rieff's first world is the world of pre-Christian paganism: the world of ancient Canaan, Babylon, Persia, Greece, and Rome, and of the aforementioned Germanic pagans (my ancestors) whom Boniface ministered to.[4] This was a world where social order is bound up in the sacred and transcendent. The will of the gods, which, although not fully in conformity

2. Aaron Renn, "Welcome to Negative World" The American Reformer, August 4, 2021, https://americanreformer.org/2021/08/welcome-to-the-negative-world-why-we-need-american-reformer.
3. Carl Trueman, *The Rise and Triumph of the Modern Self: Cultural Amnesia, Expressive Individualism, and the Road to Sexual Revolution.* (Wheaton, IL: Crossway, 2020), 74ff.
4. You could call this collective group of pre-Christian people who make up Rieff's first-world "the stoicheic order" as Peter Leithart applies Galatians 4:3 "under the elements of the world (stoicheia)" in his *Delivered from the Elements of the World: Atonement, Justification, Mission* (Downers Grove, IL: IVP Academic, 2016).

with reality as second-world (essentially Christianity) is, it grounds social order in a moral framework that mostly runs with, and not against, the Triune God's created order. The third world in Reiff's paradigm is one where the sacred and transcendent has been entirely banished. It is a wholly materialistic world. It is a world where there is no foundation whatsoever for any social order. It is the world where, to quote the philosopher Alasdair MacIntyre, the enlightenment project of justifying morality had to fail.[5] There is nothing that undergirds it. Or as one of my teachers often put it, it is a world floating in the air, as if suspended there by an enormous S-64 skycrane helicopter. Only the fading cultural memory of Christendom is holding this world together, and as the ways of Christendom are forcibly eradicated from public consciousness, that skycrane helicopter is struggling to stay airborne—we are on the verge of truly monstrous horrors, and truthfully, we have already arrived. Whether you want to call it Negative World, third world, or Trashworld, this is the world you now inhabit.

In Trueman's excellent *Rise and Triumph of the Modern Self*, he, like Renn, struggles to point to a coherent strategy for Christians. His threefold personal suggestion, which does not differ much from Dreher's (who wrote the foreword) is this: reflect on the connection between aesthetics and our core beliefs and practices, be

---

5. Alasdair MacIntyre, *After Virtue: A Study in Moral Theory*, 3rd. Ed. (Notre Dame, IN: University of Notre Dame Press, 2007), 51.

a community, recover both the natural law and a high view of the body.[6] None of these suggestions is bad, and, in fact they have quite a bit of overlap with what I have suggested in the earlier chapters of this book. We should indeed not be swayed by what Trueman calls aesthetic-based logic, or emotional appeals over and against rational argumentation. The church absolutely *must* consciously exist as a community or, as Peter Leithart calls it, an alternative polis, an alternative city within the cities of men.[7] And I also agree with Trueman that the church should recover the learning of our ancestors, how they showed the conformity between rationally deduced observations of reality and the truths of scripture. I agree with him that we should reject the pietistic gnosticism that has engulfed much of modern evangelicalism that leaves us totally vulnerable to utopian transhumanism of Trashworld, and fully embrace the physical reality of the world that God has made. But this simply will not be enough. All of these things can be done in Dreher's neo-Benedictine monastery. But Trashworld is not going to allow you to retreat to the monastery.

The single greatest problem with *The Benedict Option*, is that there is nowhere left to run. Globohomo is totalizing. Globohomo seeks to dominate every square inch of the planet. The answer is not to run and hide and await martyrdom. The answer is a Christianity that is equally

---

6. Trueman, *Rise and Triumph of the Modern Self*, 402–407.
7. Peter Leithart, *Against Christianity*, (Moscow, ID: Canon Press, 2003), 25–27ff.

aggressive and expansionary. Jesus Christ commanded His church to make disciples of *all* the nations, baptizing them and teaching them all that He has commanded to do (Matt. 28:18–20). Trashworld is a bizzaro version of the Great Commission, one that seeks to repudiate the Christian discipleship of the nations, to cast off their baptism, and to subvert all that Christ has commanded. This is not something you *can* run and hide from.

Given the cultural milieu of ostensibly conservative American Christianity in the last century, it is understandable that very bright men like Trueman and Dreher are totally befuddled about the way forward. We are discipled in a passive-aggressive, emasculated, individualistic, consumeristic, therapeutic Christianity that abhors confrontation of any kind. It should come as no surprise that "Why don't we just fight back?" is a thought that has not even remotely crossed the mind of our most important social critics. We are taught to believe that the bearing of Jesus Christ, and the bearing that we therefore as Christians must adopt, is that of Fred Rogers of *Mister Rogers' Neighborhood*. The Christian man must always be calm, friendly, and, above all else, nonconfrontational. That is what it means to be Christlike, according to contemporary evangelicalism. But this of course runs contrary to the actual Jesus Christ as He is presented in the Gospels. Yes, Jesus was the very model of patience and kindness to those who were in desperate need of grace and mercy, but nearly everywhere He went He also faced incredibly hostile opposition that He manfully and assertively confronted. Contemporary American Christianity loves the sweetness and gentleness of Jesus, but has rejected His fierceness and ferocity, almost redacting it from the Bible.

I can give you an illustration of this. Universities are a window into the future of a people about fifteen years down the road. When I was in college fifteen years ago, despite not having the vocabulary to articulate what negative-world or Trashworld was, it was very clear on campus we were living in it. I was involved in a very large, ostensibly conservative evangelical campus ministry. Every day, my large friend group from that ministry would occupy the same spot in the Student Union where we would hang out between classes. One day, as I was returning from a history class[8], all of our friends sitting in our hangout spot were noticeably agitated and abuzz. "Did you hear what [one of my closest friends] did? It was so *unChristlike!*" I was told. Everyone was furious with one of my best friends who had according to them "*badly damaged our Christian witness.*"

This is what my friend had done: NARAL or some other group advocating the murder of babies had set up a promotional table in the Student Union where we normally sat. He saw this and became incensed. He, being a student of the college of business (who paid slightly higher tuition but had access to unlimited free color printing), proceeded to print off thousands of full-color

---

8. Almost certainly a lecture about how the oppressive patriarchy forced women in colonial America to churn butter.

pictures of aborted babies, walked over to their table and scattered them everywhere, sending the pro-aborts into a flurry, hastily trying to pick them all up and hide them as he exclaimed, "THIS IS WHAT YOU PEOPLE BELIEVE IN. YOU LOVE KILLING BABIES!" Despite having just almost perfectly reenacted Jesus driving out the money-changers in the temple, all of our evangelical Christian friends who witnessed this were furious with him. They, like the evangelicalism they were formed by, believed you can "nice" people, who utterly hate everything having to do with the Christian religion, into believing in Christianity. I also told my friend that I was angry with him, and, knowing me, he was a bit taken aback.

"Yes, I am angry with you that you went and did that by yourself instead of waiting for me to be there with you!"

This episode made it clear to me from that day forward that the kind of public approach that has dominated conservative evangelical Christianity could not survive what I now call Trashworld. The only thing that emasculated, non-confrontational, neutral-world Christianity can do is do everything it can to make the Christian religion palatable to the bugman. It is why you will have pathetic appeals to "human flourishing" by people like Tim Keller when faced with a world where chopping the penises off little boys and breasts off little girls is something in the mainstream. It is why you have incessant appeals to "finding the gospel" in the inane pop culture of bugworld such as *Marvel* or *Harry Potter*.

CONCLUSION

But no matter what you do, apart from the supernatural work of the Holy Spirit, Christianity will *never* be appealing to the bugman, because Trashworld has formed and shaped the bugman to exist entirely in opposition to the Christian way of life. Genuine, biblical Christianity can appeal to the bugman no better than garlic or a crucifix can to a vampire—his entire being is formed to be in opposition to it.

The only way forward is the Boniface Option. Trashworld must be aggressively confronted and opposed. The denizens of Trashworld, the small-souled bugman, who exists entirely to consume product in his pod until he dies, are fundamentally a cowardly people. The reasons, as I have shown above, are both biological and social. They can easily manipulate the neutral-world Christian, who foolishly believes they can make Christianity appealing to the bugman if they are exceedingly agreeable. This very fact is why evangelical Christianity has rapidly succumbed to the supporters of things like homosexuality and mass migration. As the popular meme says, "No I'm not a christian and I have nothing but contempt for your backward religious beliefs, so yeah, this argument wouldn't work on me but maybe if I use it on you, you'll do what I want."

The Christianity of even sagacious men, such as Trueman and Dreher, has no answer for this. Even though they understand we are living in Negative World, they do not understand that bugmen are incapable of operating in good faith. There is nothing meaningful we hold in common with them from which we can form mutual understanding. We cannot act like Paul on Mars Hill pointing out the altar to the unknown god in Acts 17. Globohomo believes in nothing; it has no Areopagus, much less an altar to the unknown god. What they believe is undergirded by nothing. Trying to argue with a bugman from first principles is like trying to grab hold of vapor, like trying to shepherd the wind. There simply is nothing there.

Instead, you must do what Jesus did when opposing those who are incapable of acting in good faith—you hold them in derision. *That* is Christlike. When Jesus dealt with chief priests, scribes, Pharisees, and Sadducees, He knew these men were not sincere, and He was under no obligation to pretend that they were. What did He do instead? He confronted them. He rebuked them. He even mocked them. You must understand, He was not crucified for no reason. Despite what contemporary emasculated evangelicalism would tell you, He was not crucified because He was so obnoxiously nice to everyone. He was crucified because He was a threat to them. He was crucified because He directly confronted them. In negative world, this is precisely the strategy we must adopt. We must learn to become *truly* Christlike, to confront the great evils and disgusting idolatries of our day manfully and with great passion and intensity, and also to show kindness and gentleness to those suffering the most from the horrors of Trashworld.

The Personal Call

What does it look like for you personally to confront these great evils and to chop down the great oaken shrines of bugworld? The way forward will look different for each person, but there a few things I suggest:

You must honestly and accurately recognize where we currently are politically, culturally, and economically. You live in a dying apostate empire, an empire that is a wounded dying wild beast. It will not die quietly and will tear apart anything that threatens it. The regime that rules over you is filled with incompetent midwits—but this does not mean they are not dangerous. If anything, it means they are *extremely* dangerous. They have massive power that they can wield against you, but you must not fear. Instead, you must recognize the strength of your enemy that you know exactly what you must overcome.

The greatest practical need of the present is to restore an ethos of Christendom from a grassroots way. We cannot expect the orange billionaire to appear and to descend on his escalator to restore Christian civilization. His tumultuous term as president showed just how entrenched the regime is and how even the most modest attempt at reform, setting the clock back to merely mid-'90s-era liberalism, was resisted with ferocious religious zeal. Electing the right president is not going to fix things. Appointing the right Supreme Court justices is not going to fix things. Electing the right Congressmen and Senators is not going to fix things. The only thing that will transform the United States of America and pull it out of its death spiral is continual reformation of the church and revival of the Christian religion in our country and the West as a whole. And this starts with you, in your home, with your family, and extends upward from there.

This reformation and revival must begin with individual men in churches and local communities. The work has to be done. The first Christendom did not simply happen as a result of the inexorable forces of history moving. It happened because men like Saint Boniface worked to build it. The new Christendom is no different. There is much work to be done, but most of even conservative evangelical churches are content with merely managing decline.

If the Trump years, punctuated by the 2016 and 2020 elections, tell us anything, it is that there is a hunger among the population of America for a savior. Everyone who voted for that man could feel the palpable decline of America, even if they could not articulate it. There are tens of millions of Americans who simply want a normal, stable, healthy society. They want to live in a place that doesn't sexually groom kindergarteners. They want somewhere that doesn't lock them in their homes over an extremely bad seasonal flu. They want a society that doesn't reduce their existence to economic data points. They are people who were born into a proud country, a once-Christian country, who have seen that glory depart. Tens of millions of people being dispossessed by an occupying class that hates them. Tens of millions of people the church has either refused to evangelize or disciple entirely, or evangelized into a tepid, consumeristic Christian faith. The great mass of Middle America is a field ripe for the harvest. One of the greatest encumbrances to evangelizing America over the last two generations is the American peoples' love of comfort with its monocultural ubiquity. To quote Cotton Mather, "Religion begat prosperity and the daughter devoured the mother." The postwar prosperity of America is unlike what any nation has ever experienced in human history. It is no coincidence that by whatever metric you might measure—including church attendance, surveys of religious belief, tolerance of abominable practices within society, statistics of out-of-wedlock births, abortion—faithfulness has correspondingly declined with increased prosperity. As economic and cultural decline steepens, tens of millions of American men think about their situation, saying to themselves, "I work as hard as I can as many hours as I can. I am still not half as well off as my parents or grandparents were at my age. On top of that, this sick, disgusting culture wants to groom my children into trannies. Something needs to change."

Within such an environment, there is massive opportunity. This is Germania waiting for Thor's Oak to fall. The fake, disgusting Trashworld that they worship needs only one swing of the ax to come crumbling down. And bold, courageous men filled with unquenchable fire of God's Spirit can take up this call and accomplish this. It does not take many men to achieve great things for the kingdom of God. Just twelve apostles began the evangelization of the wealthiest and most powerful empire that had ever existed in human history. Do you not think God can accomplish the same thing again? He used commercial fishermen and a tax-farming thug to conquer the civilized world. Do you not think He can fill you with that same fire from His Spirit, the same power, the same passion, the same boldness?

The main difference is that we lack the courage and fire of our spiritual predecessors. We are not courageous enough to truly hate the things we ought to hate, nor bold enough to love the things we ought to love. We become seduced by the harlotries of the Trashworld we must hate. This world attacks and seeks to quench the fire that is within you at every turn. You must see Donar's Oaks everywhere that need to be felled. And you must summon the will to fell them. With men of great passion and desire, led by the Spirit of God you will see empires set aflame.

It is men like this, men like Saint Boniface, who can reach the tens of millions of our countrymen who are blindly groping in the dark for a savior. It will take courage and bravery to desecrate the high places of American idolatry. People do not want the temples of their gods plundered. But when those shrines are in ashes, they will worship the Living God in churches built on top of them. Christendom can be reforged. Christendom *will* *be* reforged.

But today it remains in ruins. And atop those ruins sits an evil, demonic regime. A regime whose adherents control every institution in public life—the massive, permanent government, every major media company, most corporations, all of academia, and even most churches. An all-encompassing ideology dominates most of the population and they are totally unaware of just how much sway it holds over them.

The way forward must be building parallel institutions and from those positions of strength recapturing institutions we have lost. The fatal flaw of the Benedict Option is that globohomo is not going to allow you hide away in your intentional community. This was true of the original monasteries, as well. The monasteries could not have survived without the protection of powerful and violent men like Clovis, the first king of what is now France, and a pagan convert to Christianity, who is famously said to have cried out when he first was told the story of Christ's crucifixion, "If I had been there with my valiant Franks, I would have avenged Him!" The need of the hour is to raise up men not only like Boniface, but also like Clovis.

You have it within your power to produce both kinds of men. You have it within your power even to be one. One of the great beauties of the American system, and the single-greatest reason we have not yet succumbed to the Chinese-style despotism that has cropped up in places like Australia and New Zealand, is that political power is widely dispersed in the United States. Who you elect as your sheriff, your county prosecutor, your mayor and city council, and your county commissioners matters a great deal. With sufficient effort, unless you live in the bluest places of America, anyone can be elected as a state representative and to the state senate. No matter how small your sphere of influence is, you or one of your friends can take over such offices and begin to fill local bureaucracies with those loyal to Christendom. It can be done, and it will be done, but it will take a tremendous amount of work and sacrifice. But as the great upheavals, which are certain to come as this revolting world continues its collapse, happen, we will need whatever legitimate sources of authority we can claim to rally and eventually build around.

These sources of authority are not limited to *political* authority alone. We have seen in recent years so many of our most trusted institutions burn through trust they had acquired over many generations. For example, a substantial portion of the population will never trust the medical establishment again for as long as they live. The same goes for the media and academia—and for good reason! As the decline hastens, trust will be the coin of the realm. Those who are willing to speak costly truths out loud will have far more credibility than those with impeccable institutional credentials who repeat lies. This heuristic will reign over any and all domains, including within the church. The new, parallel institutions that will be formed out of the ashes of the old will be led by bold truth-tellers with skin in the game. Authority will flow to those who stick their necks out for the truth. You must strive to become one of these people.

More than anything else, you must not allow the idolatries of Trashworld to bring you to shame. The great weapon globohomo is wielding against you is your desperation for social approval. If you have three to five close friends with whom you share an adamantine bond, who you trust with your life and who are totally aligned with all you hold dear, all of bugworld can rage against you, and it will not matter. If Trashworld makes you feel alone, that is when it can crush you. It is designed to make you feel as if nearly all of the world believes you are the greatest scum on earth, but you must take heart: the reality is that nearly all of humanity that has ever existed would be disgusted and revolted by the things the bugman cherishes.

This is the challenge and also the encouragement of the reformer and iconoclast in this repulsive age: we live in a ten-thousand-acre field pocked with holes where one hundred years ago there once were dozens of Chesterton's fences. And nearly every argument that was made by those opposed to tearing down the fences back when they stood, every explanation of all the things that would happen if we took down the fences, has now been totally vindicated. The great challenge is to show a deluded world the obvious truths that they deny. The encouragement is that reality has proven us right and it will continue to do so.

Jesus Christ has given His people the command to make all the nations into His disciples and He has promised to be with us as we do this. He did not give us this command expecting us to fail. He did not send His church on a suicide mission that was doomed from the outset. As you spend your life conquering (or reconquering) space for the kingdom of Jesus Christ, just as Saint Boniface marched into Germania, He has promised He will be with you and He will never forsake you.

Go forth and conquer.

We are going to win.

Acknowledgments

There are so many people I wish to thank. A project like this is the culmination of not just my own work but the support and encouragement of very many people, not all of whom I will even be able to name.

To my friend Andrew Torba, thank you for making this book possible and helping in so many uncountable ways, I will never be able to repay him in this lifetime. You are true friend and closer than a brother to me!

To Jake McAtee, who originally got me started on this work and spurred me to actually get what I had to say on paper. I look forward to enjoying some Wooster's pies very soon. One bite. Everybody knows the rules.

To Brian Kohl, whose editorial acumen is absolutely top notch. This book would not be what it is without your labors.

To Richard Osgar, my editor at Gab News, whose countless hours working with me on this got this across the finish line. I might have taken years off your life, but I hope you are as proud of this work as I am!

To Valerie Bost, who is a copyediting and typesetting wizard and a good friend. You have made this book a pleasure to read.

To Joel Jeffrey, whose narration work is so extremely good. Thank you for making this book a pleasure to listen to.

To Santiago Pliego and John Mansfield, whose encouragement and excitement over the book kept me pumped up throughout it all. You may have made me better understand what my wife has gone through with each pregnancy, when she looks ready to pop, and everyone keeps asking her, "When's that baby coming?" Yes, the book is finally out!

To all my frens in the group chat, you know who you are, and you should know how much your support means to me. So much of this work is the collection of conversations online, and with people I will never meet in person or even know their real names—the internet is a crazy, awesome place.

To Peder, Dean, Jon, Justin, and Brandon, your friendship means the world to me.

And lastly, and most importantly, thank you to my wife, Kara, who is somehow even more thrilled about this book going to print than I am. Thank you for always being there for me and understanding the long hours and focus this kind of thing requires and being eager to help in any way you can. I will be forever thankful for you.

Made in United States
Orlando, FL
25 August 2023